create your

MOBILE HOT DOG CART COMPANY

Steven Primm, CPA

Tim Roncevich, CISA

UPSTART
Business Consulting Group

www.upstartbcg.com

Hot Dog Cart Company

© 2007 by Upstart Business Consulting Group
www.upstartbcg.com
All rights reserved. No part of this publication may be reproduced, be stored electronically, be stored in a retrieval system, or transmitted in any form or by any means, electronic, mechanical, photocopying, recording, scanning, or otherwise, except as permitted under Sections 107 or 108 of the 1976 United States Copyright Act without permission of the copyright owner.

Limit of liability and disclaimer or warranty: The publisher and the authors make no representations or warranties with respect to the accuracy or completeness of the contents of this business plan kit and specifically disclaim all warranties, including without limitation warranties for a particular purpose. No warranty may be created or extended by sales or promotional materials. The advice and strategies contained herein may not be suitable for every situation. This work is sold with the understanding that the publisher is not engaged in rendering legal, accounting, or other professional services. If professional assistance is required, the services of a competent professional should be sought. Neither the publisher nor the authors shall be liable for damages arising herein. The fact that an organization or website is referred to in the work as a citation and/or a potential source of further information does not mean that the publisher or authors endorse the information the organization or website may provide or recommendations it may make. Further, readers should be aware that websites listed in this work may have changed or disappeared between when this work was written and when it is read.

Printed in the United States of America

Contents

Introduction 7
Executive Summary 9
   Company 9
   Description of Product and Service 9
   Market 9
   Financial Profile 10
   Funds Needed and Use of Proceeds 10
Summary Description of the Business 11
   Mission Statement 11
   Business Model 11
   Strategy 11
   Strategic Relationships 12
   SWOT Analysis 14
      Strengths: 15
      Weaknesses: 15
      Opportunities: 15
      Threats: 16
Product and Service 17
   Product Process 17
   Service Process 17
Location 19
Legal Structure 21
   Type of Legal Structure 21
   Choosing a Legal Structure 26
   List of Owners and/or Corporate Officers 26
Personnel 27
   List of Key Personnel 27
   Personnel Responsibilities 27
   Personnel Compensation 27
Independent Contractors vs. Employees 29
   Employees 29
   Independent Contractors 29
   Necessary Qualifications 31
   Job Descriptions 32
   Expected Hours 32
   Adding Employees and Independent Contractors 33

Accounting Software	**35**
Legal	**37**
Insurance	**39**
Security	**41**
Overview and Goals of Marketing Strategy	**43**
Market Analysis	**45**
Target Market	45
Competition	47
Market Trends	47
Market Research	47
Marketing Strategy	**49**
General Description	49
Advertising Strategy	49
Pricing	52
Brand	52
Database Marketing	53
Sales Strategy	53
Sales Incentives and Promotions	53
Public Relations	54
Networking	54
Customer Service	**57**
Description of Customer Service Activities	57
Expected Outcomes of Achieving Excellence	57
Implementation of Marketing Strategy	**59**
In-house Responsibilities	59
Outsourced Functions	59
Assessment of Marketing Effectiveness	**61**
Financial Documents	**63**
Financial Needs – Startup Expenses	63
Loan Dispersal Statement	64
Credit Policy	64
Business Bank Account	65
Break-even Analysis	**67**
Tax Considerations	**69**
Income Tax	69
Self-employment Tax	69
Employment Tax	70
Excise Tax	70
Business License	70

Outsourced Tax Functions 71
Three Year Income Statement Projection 73
Three Year Balance Sheet Projection 77
Three Year Cash Flow Projection 81
Additional Forecasting Charts 85
Supporting Documents 87
    Personal Resumes 87
    Owners Financial Statements 87
    Credit Reports 87
    Copies of Leases, Mortgages, and other Agreements 88
    Letters of Reference 88
    Contracts 88
    Other Legal Documents 88
    Miscellaneous Documents 88
Appendix A: Financial Ratios 89
Appendix B: Helpful Websites 91
Appendix C: Business Template Instructions 93
Appendix D: Glossary 95

Introduction

This business plan kit is directly related to your freedom, your personal and financial freedom. Whether you are retired, currently working, or a recent college graduate, this business plan kit provides valuable information for starting a hot dog cart company. This business plan kit is for those individuals who:
- Are passionate about owning a hot dog cart company
- Want a better work/life balance
- Want the flexibility of running their own business
- Want the pride and fulfillment that comes with owning their own business and being an entrepreneur
- Want to earn extra income
- Want to be their own boss

Upstart Business Consulting Group has created this comprehensive business plan kit so you have the tools necessary to pursue your dreams, being an entrepreneur in the United States of America. This kit will guide you through the critical aspects of creating your own business plan for your company. We only create business plan kits for start-up businesses that can capitalize on current trends based on consumer demand across the United States. All businesses we cover require an initial start-up capital investment of $1,000 to $10,000. Although the required start-up capital is relatively small, you will have the potential for substantial cash flow. The format of this business plan kit is modeled after business plans that have been used in successful start-up companies.

This business plan kit:
- Outlines your business from its creation to the daily operation, all in an easy to understand format
- Was written by successful entrepreneurs and business consultants
- Includes useful information to help you avoid the typical pitfalls that are common in starting your own business
- Includes access to free business templates to help you get your new business started

- Helps you decide on the right legal structure for your new business
- And much more useful information that you need to know when starting your new business

Perhaps the greatest resource this business plan kit provides is the ability for you to e-mail your questions to professional business consultants and entrepreneurs from Upstart Business Consulting Group. Whatever your question may be, you will find a competent resource available to help you.

We know that you will find this business plan kit useful in achieving your goal of personal and financial freedom while building a business you love.

Executive Summary

Company

Your hot dog cart company will be the leader in both customer service and quality hot dogs. You will focus your efforts on building strategic relationships between party planners, catering employees, friends, and family. You will offer the highest value hot dogs at a competitive price in your market, allowing controlled and sustainable growth.

Description of Product and Service

Your hot dog cart company will offer high quality hot dogs. All hot dogs will be purchased from a reputable wholesaler to ensure quality assurance. Your hot dog cart will sell products at local fairs, sporting events, and other local community events.

If needed to delegate tasks, you will hire independent contractors to assist you in various aspects of your business. The duties you assign may include picking up ingredients and staffing the hot dog cart at various events. The duties you delegate will be determined by the level of business activity and the company's ability to support additional expenses.

Market

Great tasting hot dogs are extremely popular at sporting events and other community events. Individuals and companies are willing to pay a premium for great tasting hot dogs that add a special element and authenticity to their party or event. Your target market includes events held by individuals (birthdays, anniversaries, reunions, special occasions, etc.), corporate parties (holiday party, birthday, promotion celebration, etc.), and other events. Individuals who purchase your hot dogs will likely be making impulse buying decisions, thus allowing you to charge a premium for your product.

Financial Profile

Financial projections should be based on similar companies in your geographic region. Your price point will be slightly higher than these companies. Below is a chart listing key performance indicators for the first three years of operation (based on income statements figures within the business plan):

Key Indicator	Year 1	Year 2	Year 3
Total Revenue	$20,918	$31,378	$47,066
Gross Margin	$14,403	$21,184	$32,166
Operating Income	$11,223	$18,275	$29,257
Net Income	$7,407	$12,062	$19,310

Funds Needed and Use of Proceeds

Your hot dog cart company will need about $6,000 in startup funding. A detailed list of equipment and budget information is listed below in the Financial Needs – Startup Funding section later in this kit. Funding will consist of personal savings from the owner/s. The proceeds will be used to pay for equipment, recipes, packaging, insurance, and marketing expenditures. Future growth will be funded through the company's positive cash flow or through the use of credit cards. Additional capital from new investors will not be used due to the high cost associated with this type of financing.

Summary Description of the Business

Mission Statement

A mission statement formally declares what your company is trying to achieve in the medium to long term. Your mission statement should be market oriented and defined by your product or service (e.g. "We sell high quality hot dogs"). You should avoid making your mission too narrow or too broad. Your mission should be realistic and should not be used for public relations purposes, but instead be specific with workable guidelines. A good market oriented mission statement should sound like this: "We sell tasty, high quality hot dogs in convenient locations and provide the best customer service."

Business Model

The business model defines how you plan to execute your mission statement. Your company needs to provide your target market the highest quality hot dogs and have superior customer service. Since you may have competition in the area, the combination of quality hot dogs and great service will enable long term growth and success.

Strategy

The strategy of your hot dog cart company should consist of the following:
- Attract profitable customers who value the quality hot dogs and convenience your cart provides. Do not try to win new business by being the low price leader. Charge a fair price and emphasize your quality service and quality ingredients.
- Provide the highest value to your customers. This means providing the highest quality products and services at a price customers are willing to pay. For private events, do not try to "nickel and dime" your customers for short term profit. Instead, focus on pleasing the customer to ensure a long term relationship and positive word of mouth. This type of strategy will enable long term growth and higher profit margins.

- Grow the business in a smart way. Before spending too much money through purchasing additional equipment, be sure there will not be cash flow restraints that may be harmful to the business. If possible, employ bootstrap financing. Bootstrap financing is a collection of finance methods used to minimize the amount of outside debt and equity financing needed from banks and investors. Bootstrap financing requires the entrepreneur to start the business with as little capital as possible early in the life of the business in order to generate positive cash flow as soon as possible. Bootstrap financing methods include personal savings, credit cards, second mortgages, and friends/family.
- Create a special style or image to differentiate yourself from your competitors. Research other hot dog cart companies and find a way to make your product better.
- Network and create key contacts within the party planning industry. Create a commission structure of 5% to 10% of individual party revenue to create an incentive for party planners to refer business to your company.
- Build the business through word of mouth referrals. Word of mouth is the passing of information by verbal means, especially recommendations, in an informal, person-to-person manner. Word of mouth is not only the most credible form of marketing, but it is also the least expensive. Subscribe to the Word of Mouth Marketing newsletter to gain insight on word of mouth marketing techniques (*www.womma.org*).

When properly applied, the above business strategy should allow for sustained growth and early positive cash flow to fund future growth.

Strategic Relationships

Strategic relationships should consist of the following individuals and groups:
- Party Planners: party planners would not be in business if they did not have high quality vendors to choose from to outsource work. Hot dogs are extremely popular at sporting events, family reunions, and other special events. You should build

the relationship to become the preferred hot dog cart provider for party planners. A 5% to 10% commission is also a great incentive to entice party planners to use your company. When a party planner does use your service, you must fulfill your promise of providing the highest level of product and service to ensure the relationship between the party planner and your company endures.

- Previous Customers: past customers provide the most credible word of mouth. Continually build the relationship with your customers, preferably by e-mail or telephone. Send cards for customer birthdays, anniversaries, or just to say hello. Cards are also an effective way to notify past customers about your upcoming promotions.
- Complementary Businesses: complementary businesses consist of other types of businesses who serve the same market as your company but are not direct competitors (e.g. beverages cart companies, ice cream cart companies, cotton candy cart companies, etc.). In addition to giving complementary businesses a commission, you should also refer your customers to their company. This will give your customers the opportunity to purchase goods and services from the complementary business. This is a win-win for both your company and complementary businesses. In order to gain the trust of complementary businesses, you must provide high quality service at a fair price.
- Hotel Sales and Catering Managers: hotel sales and catering managers build their business through repeat customers. If you provide high quality products and services at a fair price, the hotel sales and catering managers will have satisfied customers. With satisfied customers, the hotel sales and catering managers will be extremely pleased because they have worked hard to build the relationship with their customers. Providing high quality products and services should make you the preferred hot dog cart vendor. Additionally, a 5% to 10% commission is also a great incentive to entice hotel sales and catering managers to use your company. Although the hotel sales and catering managers may not be able to accept a

commission due to a conflict of interest, it is always best to offer the incentive as goodwill.
- Managers of Fairs, Swap Meets, and other Local Festivals: this is a great opportunity to gain exposure in your community. If you can create a relationship with the managers of fairs, swap meets, and other local festivals, they may be able to move your booth to a higher traffic area for little to no cost. As with real estate, one key to success at these types of events is location, location, location. The better your booth location means higher foot traffic and more sales.
- Banquet Facility Managers: just like hotel sales and catering manager, banquet facility managers build their business by repeat customers. If you provide high quality products and services at a fair price, the banquet facility managers will have satisfied customers. With satisfied customers, the banquet facility managers will be extremely pleased because they have worked hard to build the relationship with their customers. Providing high quality products and services should make you the preferred hot dog cart vendor. Additionally, a 5% to 10% commission is also a great incentive to entice banquet facility managers to use your company. Although the banquet facility managers may not be able to accept a commission due to a conflict of interest, it is always best to offer the incentive as goodwill

Ensure that your contact information is clearly displayed on your hot dog cart and your business cards/flyers are available whenever your hot dog cart is rented.

SWOT Analysis

The SWOT Analysis is used to identify your company's Strengths, Weaknesses, Opportunities, and Threats in order to identify a strategic niche that your company can exploit. By understanding these components and how they apply to your business, you should be able to improve operations and strategies in many areas to grow and sustain your profitability. We recommend you complete a SWOT analysis every 12-18 months. Below is a sample SWOT analysis that you can use to guide your own SWOT analysis:

Strengths:
- Creativity: Be creative when marketing your hot dog cart. You need to differentiate your company from others in the same industry.
- Customer service: Provide the best customer service in the industry to separate your company from all others.

Weaknesses:
- Do not have established reputation in the food cart industry.
- Entrenched competitors with established brand and customer base may have a large percentage of the market (see "*Opportunities*" section below).
- Low barriers to entry include low start up capital and new competitors with a large network who can easily sell hot dogs to their existing network.

Opportunities:
- Create strategic relationships with party planners, catering managers, banquet facility managers, and corporations. These strategic relationships will lead to repeat business and sustained long term growth.
- If there is a large competitor, you have the opportunity to come in and take market share. Your unique combination of high quality products, great customer service, and differentiation will create raving customers who will generate positive word of mouth.
- Positive cash flow can be expected after the first several months of sales.
- The popularity of hot dog carts for special events and sporting events is growing rapidly.
- Low cost, entry level business for the upstart entrepreneur. You will need about $6,000 to start the business.

Threats:
- Growth may be rapid, but must be controlled. Do not purchase additional equipment or other expensive items until sufficient cash flow can be generated to pay for such purchases.
- New competition undercuts your prices. However, if you create a strong customer base and solid word of mouth of marketing, you will not have to worry about your customers going with another company for a lower price. Trust breeds loyalty, and loyal customers are great for long term growth. Customer loyalty is what separates successful companies from unsuccessful companies.

Product and Service

Product Process

High quality hot dog cart products include:
- Quarter pound beef franks
- Quarter pound kosher dogs
- Veggie dogs
- Turkey dogs
- Whole wheat buns
- Variety of bagged chips
- Variety of bottled soda and water
- Large variety of condiments and toppings including ketchup, mustard, relish, peppers, chili, celery salt, tomatoes, kraut, cheddar cheese, and onions

Since you are selling a food product, make sure you comply with the proper food safety regulations that are set forth by the Center for Food Safety and Applied Nutrition "CFSAN" (part of the Food and Drug Administration). You can perform online research through the CSFAN website (http://www.cfsan.fda.gov/list.html) to ensure you are complying and adhering to the proper regulations.

Service Process

Professional, energetic, and knowledgeable owners and employees are what create raving customers. High quality service will determine if your company will be successful or unsuccessful. Great tasting hot dogs and unparalleled service are by far the most important elements of your business strategy. You may want to include a 100% satisfaction guarantee with your products to give your customers the assurance that you stand behind your products. Shipments and deliveries should be made when promised.

Location

A hot dog cart company is the perfect home based business. We highly recommend you use a home office to run your business, not only for the tax benefits, but also for the overhead cost savings. The majority of the equipment should be housed in your company trailer. Excess equipment can be housed in your garage. If you have any local ordinances that prevent you from storing the trailer in your driveway, you can rent a parking space at your local storage facility for a small monthly fee.

Legal Structure

Type of Legal Structure

Below is a brief description of the major types of legal structures you may choose to form. Following the description, there will be a handy chart that will give you a brief snapshot of the pros, cons, and tax rules for each legal structure.

- Sole Proprietorship: A sole proprietorship is a one person business that is not registered with the state. You do not have to do anything special or file any papers to set up a sole proprietorship. You create a sole proprietorship just by going into business for yourself. Legally, a sole proprietorship is inseparable from its owner (i.e. the business and the owner are one and the same). This means the owner of the business reports business income and losses on his or her personal tax return and is personally liable for any business related obligations, such as debts or court judgments. Your income tax return for this business is filed on Schedule C of your individual form 1040. Self-employment taxes (i.e. the employer and employee's share of FICA taxes) are to be paid upon all earnings from a sole proprietorship in addition to standard income taxes. If your business operates under a trade name (e.g. On-The-Run Hot Dogs), you must file a fictitious business name registration with the county in which you will be operating. However, there will be no state franchise taxes due. In California, for example, the minimum annual franchise tax for corporations is $800 per year. However, most other states have annual franchise taxes under $100. Refer to your state franchise tax board for additional information.

    Sole proprietorships make sense in a business where personal liability is not a big worry (e.g. a small service business in which you are unlikely to be sued and for which you will not be borrowing much money for inventory or other costs).

- Partnership: A partnership is simply a business owned by two or more people that have not filed papers to become a corporation or a limited liability company (LLC). You do not have to file any paperwork to form a partnership. The partnership arrangement begins as soon as you start a business with another person. As in a sole proprietorship, the partnership's owners pay taxes on their share of the business income on their personal tax returns. Partners are each personally liable for the entire amount of any business debts and claims. Also, each partner has the potential to hold all partners liable for actions taken in connection with the business. To avoid future feuds and confusion, a partnership should have a written partnership agreement that spells out the rights and duties of the partners relative to partnership assets, liabilities, income (loss), and control of business operations. Refer to the sample partnership agreement on the template page of the UBCG website. Partnerships file a separate tax return on federal form 1041 and partners pay Social Security and Medicare on all partnership earnings.

    Partnerships make sense in a business where personal liability is not a big worry (e.g. a small service business in which you and your partners are unlikely to be sued and for which you will not be borrowing much money for inventory or other costs).

- Limited Liability Company (LLC): An LLC is formed through the filing of articles of organization with the appropriate state office for corporate filings (usually the Secretary of State). An LLC is a hybrid between a partnership and a corporation. Generally, LLC's are required by state law to have written operating agreements that set forth the rights and duties of the LLC members, much like a partnership agreement. Refer to the sample LLC operating agreement on the template page of the UBCG website. Although an LLC can be organized with non-member employees operating the business, the IRS has ruled that in most cases LLC members shall be liable for self-employment taxes on their share of LLC earnings. An LLC reports its income (loss) on federal form 1041. LLC members are not personally liable for the debt of an LLC. LLC's provide limited personal liability for business debts and claims. But when it comes to taxes, LLC's are more like partnerships (i.e. the owners of an LLC pay taxes on their share of the business income on their personal tax returns). The main benefit of an LLC is that these structures limit the owners' personal liability for business debts and court judgments against the business.

LLC's make sense for business owners who either 1) run the risk of being sued by customers, 2) run the risk of piling up a lot of business debt, or 3) have substantial personal assets they want to protect from business creditors.

- S-Corporation: A corporation is formed through the filing of articles of incorporation with the state. Refer to the sample articles of incorporation on the template page of the UBCG website. There is no distinction between an S-Corporation and a C-Corporation when the initial filing of the articles of incorporation is made with the state. To become an S-Corporation, a corporation must file Form 2553 with the IRS within a certain deadline to qualify for S status. If you fail to make a timely S-Corporation election, the corporation is automatically a C-Corporation. S-Corporations are taxed on income (and losses) like partnerships in that there is no entity level taxation. Please note that S-Corporations that formerly were C-Corporations can be taxed upon "built-in gains" that existed upon their conversion from C to S. Shareholders are not personally liable for the debts of S-Corporations. Employment and unemployment taxes are only paid upon the designated salary of a shareholder and not upon dividends. What sets an S-Corporation apart from all other types of businesses is that an S-Corporation is an independent legal and tax entity, separate from the people who own, control, and manage it. Because of this separate status, the owners of an S-Corporation do not use their personal tax returns to pay taxes on corporate profits. Instead, the S-Corporation itself pays these taxes. Owners pay personal income tax only on money they draw from the corporation in the form of salaries and bonuses. The main benefit of an S-Corporation is that these structures limit the owners' personal liability for business debts and court judgments against the business.

An S-Corporation makes sense for business owners who either 1) run the risk of being sued by customers, 2) run the risk of piling up a lot of business debt, or 3) have substantial personal assets they want to protect from business creditors.

- C-Corporation: A corporation is formed through the filing of articles of incorporation with the state. Refer to the sample articles of incorporation on the template page of the UBCG website. There is no distinction between an S-Corporation and a C-Corporation when the initial filing of the articles of incorporation is made with the state. If you fail to make a timely S election, the corporation is automatically a C-Corporation. C-Corporations have their income taxed at the corporate level. S-Corporations that formerly were C-Corporations can be taxed upon "built-in gains" that existed upon their conversion from C to S. Shareholders are not personally liable for the debts of C-Corporations. Employment and unemployment taxes are only paid upon the designated salary of a shareholder and not upon dividends. What sets the C-Corporation apart from all other types of businesses is that a C-Corporation is an independent legal and tax entity, separate from the people who own, control and manage it. Because of this separate status, the owners of a C-Corporation do not use their personal tax returns to pay tax on corporate profits. Instead, the C-Corporation itself pays these taxes. Owners pay personal income tax only on money they draw from the corporation in the form of salaries and bonuses. The main benefit of a C-Corporation is that these structures limit the owners' personal liability for business debts and court judgments against the business.

  A C-Corporation makes sense for business owners who either 1) run the risk of being sued by customers, 2) run the risk of piling up a lot of business debt, or 3) have substantial personal assets they want to protect from business creditors.

Type of Structure	Pros	Cons	Tax Rules
Sole Proprietorship	Simple and inexpensive to create and operate	Owner personally liable for business debts and lawsuits	Owner reports profit or loss on his or her personal tax return (schedule C of form 1040)
General Partnership	Simple and inexpensive to create and operate	Owners (partners) personally liable for business debts and lawsuits	Entity must file form 1065. Each partner receives a Schedule K with their proportion of income and expenses which is included with each individual's income tax return (form 1040)
Limited Liability Company (LLC)	Owners have limited personal liability for business debts even if they participate in management	More expensive to create than partnership or sole proprietorship

State laws for creating LLC's may not reflect latest federal tax changes | Profit and loss can be allocated differently than ownership interests

IRS rules now allow LLC's to choose between being taxed as a partnership or a corporation |
| C-Corporation and S-Corporation | Owners have limited personal liability for business debts

Fringe benefits limited for owners who own more than 2% of shares | More expensive to create than partnership or sole proprietorship

More paperwork than a Limited Liability Company (LLC), which offers similar advantages | Owners report their share of corporate profit or loss on their personal tax returns

Owners can use corporate loss to offset income from other sources. Income must be allocated to owners according to their ownership interests |

25

Choosing a Legal Structure

Most owners of hot dog cart companies will operate as a sole proprietorship, general partnership, or limited liability company. Sole proprietorships and general partnerships are the easiest and least expensive to form and tax filings are relatively simple. Limited liability companies are designed for businesses that expect to be sued from time to time and the owners want to protect their personal assets. As all individual situations are different, professional tax and legal advice is recommended if you are not sure which legal structure is right for you.

List of Owners and/or Corporate Officers

This section should list owners and how profits, losses, and expenses will be distributed. Include a list of each owner's strengths along with resumes as an appendix to the business plan. Depending on the legal structure of your company, you will need to create a partnership agreement, articles of incorporation, or LLC operating agreement. Refer to the "Type of Legal Structure" section for additional details.

Name	Title	Responsibilities	Owner (Yes/No)	Ownership % (Partnerships only)

Personnel

List of Key Personnel
This section should list key personnel who will be running or assisting in the business, if you desire one or more people to help and the size of your business warrants such personnel. Include a list of each person's strengths along with resumes as an appendix to the business plan.

Personnel Responsibilities
We recommend you hire personnel to perform limited responsibilities. As the business owner, you should be selling products, creating strategic relationships, and answering customer questions. If you have personnel perform some or all of these tasks, you risk them taking this knowledge and starting their own hot dog cart company (refer to the low barriers to entry weakness in the "SWOT Analysis" section). The duties your assign are completely up to you. Your employee should handle the following responsibilities:
- Picking up equipment from your home or trailer storage yard.
- Delivering, setting up, and breaking down all equipment required for each event.
- Being the onsite point of contact for your company. Be sure to tell your customer that you will not be onsite the day of the event but will have a capable manager onsite to handle the event.
- Picking up production ingredients as needed.
- Staffing the hot dog cart at various events.

Personnel Compensation
You may choose to pay your personnel a set hourly wage or base their pay off of a percentage of revenue the company makes. You should discuss the options with your personnel and decide which form of wage calculation they would prefer. With a set hourly wage, you can easily estimate how much your personnel will make each period.

However, there are potential tax consequences if you pay the personnel a set hourly wage.

Independent Contractors vs. Employees

Employees

Once demand allows and you have a consistent number of events per week, you will most likely be hiring employees to assist you in staffing your hot dog cart. Before you hire your first employee, you should consult with an accountant, lawyer, or a member of the Service Corp of Retired Executives (SCORE) to help assist you in the process. You want to be sure you are following all applicable local, state, and federal laws. Once you hire your first employee, the learning curve of hiring additional employees is greatly reduced.

When you have a large order or cannot attend an event yourself, try to hire personnel on a per-job basis so they can be considered independent contractors. See below for more information regarding the independent contractor relationship.

Independent Contractors

If possible, you should hire independent contractors instead of employees. The independent contractor relationship benefits both you and the independent contractors. However, you become liable for all withholding taxes and possible nonpayment penalties if the IRS reclassifies your independent contractors as employees. As a company that only hires independent contractors, you have less paperwork and are not required to do the following:
- Provide the same fringe benefits offered to employees, such as insurance coverage, vacation days, sick days, and pensions.
- Pay unemployment taxes.
- Pay half of the FICA tax.
- Pay other state and local taxes, such as unemployment and workers compensation.
- Withhold income taxes and Social Security taxes (FICA) from employee wages.

Additionally, as independent contractors, they receive the tax benefits of a self-employed businessperson, such as travel and entertainment deductions. No taxes are withheld from the earnings of independent contractors because they are responsible for the payment of their own taxes. Remember, you must complete Form 1099-MISC for your independent contractors.

The main factors that distinguish an independent contractor from an employee are whether the employer "controls" the worker and the basis upon which the worker is paid. Independent contractors are those who:
- Are paid on a commission or per-job basis (not an hourly wage).
- Do not submit oral or written reports.
- Set their own pace and the sequence of services performed.
- Pay for their own traveling expenses.
- Furnish their own tools and materials (e.g. attire).
- Provide services to the general public.
- Cannot be fired if contract specifications are met.
- Work for more than one employer or, at the very least, are not required to work full-time for one employer.
- Are hired to perform one particular job at a time and do not work for the same employer year after year.
- Do not receive any job training from the employer.
- Work on their own and decide how work is to be completed without employer direction.

If you are in doubt whether your staff members are employees or independent contractors, file Form SS-8 ("Information for Use in Determining Whether a Worker Is an Employee for Purposes of Federal Employment Taxes and Income Tax Withholding") with the IRS. Either way, make sure to take the following precautions to prevent an unfavorable audit from the IRS:
- The worker should bill you for services rendered.
- Draft a written contract that provides for and/or contains (1) the type of service to be performed, (2) the place of work, (3) payment, (4) duration of the contract, (5) an arbitration clause, and (6) a covenant against competition.

- As much independence as possible should be given to the worker (e.g. supervision on the job or the location where the work is to be performed).
- The worker should be required to provide his or her own tools, supplies, training, and transportation.

The IRS may see your managers as employees if you pay them hourly or have too much "control" over the work they complete. In order to have your managers be seen as independent contractors, you may decide to pay them on a per-job basis (e.g. percentage of revenue or profit for each party) and follow the above guidelines and precautions. Remember, having independent contractors will increase your bottom line due to the significant tax savings.

Necessary Qualifications

You need to identify the necessary qualifications that you will be looking for when hiring employees or independent contractors. You need to identify these qualifications through the use of job descriptions. Although you may want to limit the responsibilities given to your personnel listed below are descriptions for all possible positions for a hot dog cart company:

- Sales and Customer Service Representative: job responsibilities include being the main point of contact for your company. This person should make the majority of sales to the strategic partnership customers and other customers. Also, this person should contact the customer after the event to ensure all expectations were met. Job responsibilities should be completed by company owner.
- Hot Dog Cart Staffer: job responsibilities include hiring staff, terminating staff, and creating work schedules to make sure each hot dog cart is appropriately staffed. Job responsibilities should be completed by the company owner.
- Delivery and On-site Personnel: job responsibilities include delivering, setting up, and breaking down the hot dog cart and related equipment. Additionally, this position is tasked with operating the hot dog cart at fairs, sporting events, and other local community events.

Job Descriptions

Job descriptions should include the following information:
- Job Title
- Direct Report (who the worker is supposed to report to)
- General Summary
- Essential Duties and Responsibilities
- Job Specifications and Requirements
- Qualifications
- Experience
- Working Conditions
- Disclaimer (e.g. "The above statements are intended to describe the general nature and level of work being performed by people assigned to this classification. They are not intended to be construed as an exhaustive list of all responsibilities, duties, and skills required of personnel so classified")
- Approved By
- Approval Date
- Refer to the sample job description on the template page of the UBCG website.

Expected Hours
- Sales and Customer Service Representative: hours per week varies based on the demand for hot dog cart rentals. Active marketing and sales should require at least 5 to 10 hours per week.
- Hot Dog Cart Staffer: depending on how many carts you have going out on a daily or weekly basis, scheduling can take anywhere from 10 minutes to 1 hour per week. Most of the time, the work schedule will not change much from week to week. Also, expect to spend 2 hours with paperwork each time there is a new hire or termination of an employee.
- Delivery and On-site Personnel: hours per week varies based on the demand for hot dog cart rentals. For each event where the hot dog cart is booked, expect to spend 8-14 hours per day operating the cart.

Adding Employees and Independent Contractors

As your business grows and demand increases for your services, you will need additional staff (employees and independent contractors). You should never stop trying to attract new staff. The best way to attract new staff is to ask current staff if they can refer any friends. You can also post advertisements in a local newspaper, culinary school, or post advertisements on the web (e.g. Craigslist). However, when you post advertisements in newspapers and on websites, be ready to expect a high number of responses. Unfortunately, you will only have a few quality leads.

Accounting Software

Accounting for your business is a vital activity to ensure your long term success. Accurate and diligent accounting of your income and expenses will ensure you have collected past due balances from your customers and are prepared to easily file your tax return at the end of the year. Spreadsheets are helpful and the use of special accounting software makes accounting a breeze. User-friendly software, such as QuickBooks, will provide all the accounting activities and services most businesses will need. Accounting software is also easy to import into tax software (e.g. Turbo Tax). Although there are companies that provide accounting services, keeping track of your own accounting activities will allow you to keep more of your hard earned income in your own pocket.

Legal

Your company should seek legal representation on an as needed basis. For general legal questions, you may be able to rely on a friend who is an attorney. For tax-based legal questions, you can ask a Certified Public Accountant (CPA) for assistance. Before you pay an attorney, consult with your local Service Corp of Retired Executives (SCORE) counselor or local Small Business Administration (SBA) office to see if one of their consultants can answer your question at no charge. You can contact SCORE and the SBA through their respective websites (www.score.org and www.sba.gov).

Be sure to check with your local and state health departments to determine if your kitchen will meet health standards for selling food products and any necessary licenses you must obtain.

Insurance

There are several types of insurance that are recommended for this type of business:
- Trailer Insurance: you will need both liability and replacement coverage for your business truck and/or trailer.
- Content Insurance: if the trailer is stolen or the equipment that is stored within the trailer is damaged, you will need this insurance to recover the cost of the equipment.
- $1,000,000 General Liability Insurance: you will need this insurance to protect you from injuries that your workers or customers suffer at your hot dog cart.
- Disability: this insurance will provide coverage for you or your managers if you are not able to work for a specific period of time.

Consult with your current insurance provider to obtain quotes and to determine whether you need additional types of insurance coverage. Remember, before you choose coverage, shop around with other insurance brokers to find the best price. As your business grows and you acquire additional assets, consult with your insurance provider to determine if you need additional insurance coverage.

Security

Depending on how much equipment you purchase, you may be able to store all of it in your company trailer. Excess equipment that does not fit in your trailer can be stored in your garage. You may have up to $10,000 worth of equipment as your business grows, so you want to make sure your investment is secure. Whether your equipment is stored in your trailer or garage, security must be of the utmost importance. Ensure that your garage is securely locked at all times if you plan to use it as storage space. With security, an ounce of prevention is worth a pound of cure.

Overview and Goals of Marketing Strategy

If implemented properly, your marketing strategy should allow for sustained and controlled growth. The next four sections detail the key elements of your marketing strategy.

Market Analysis

Target Market
Your target market consists of the following types of groups:
- Private parties and events held by individuals:
    o The events you target include birthdays, barbeques, and other special occasions.
    o If the interested customer was referred to you by a previous customer, chances are they will be more concerned with quality service and quality hot dogs and less concerned about price. You can typically charge full price for these types of customers.
    o If the interested customer found your company through your other advertising methods (e.g. online ad, yellow pages, etc.), chances are they have contacted several other hot dog cart companies for quotes. These customers tend to be more price sensitive and may look for the lowest priced company. Explain to these customers that the price is based on the high level of service and quality hot dogs you sell. Try to convince them that even though you may charge a higher price than your competitors, your customers receive a much higher level of service. If they refuse to pay your price, you may want to drop your price slightly as a sign of goodwill and to gain the business. However, do not drop your price too much because you end up losing the high quality service image that will make your company a long term success.
- Fundraising events:
    o Fundraising groups are typically looking for the lowest priced service provider. Be sure to record all donated hot dogs to non-profits and fundraising events as these may be able to be deducted as charitable contributions in your tax return.

- Corporate events:
    - The events you target include corporate Olympics, corporate barbeques, corporate picnics, and corporate sponsored office lunch days.
    - If the interested customer was referred to you by a party planner, chances are they will be more concerned with quality products and less concerned about price. You can typically charge full price for these types of customers. If you exceed expectations, you will not only receive future business from the customer, but you will also receive future referrals from the party planner. You can build your business very fast if you have a large network of party planners that refer all events requiring a hot dog cart your way. If you give commissions to party planners, a good tip is to add the party planner commission to the price of the party. This will allow you to pass the commission expense on to the customer and retain your normal profit margin.
    - If the interested customer found your company through your other advertising methods (e.g. online ad, yellow pages, etc.), chances are high that you can still charge your full price. Once again, the customer will be more concerned with quality products less concerned about price. If you are being undercut from competitors, simply explain to the customer that they will get what they pay for. If they choose the lowest priced competitor, they will likely receive low quality service and low quality products.
- People Attending Fairs, Swap Meets, and other Local Festivals and Events: the people who attend these types of events are looking for products that cannot necessarily make at home. They are looking for tasty treats and are likely to make impulsive buying decisions. Be creative in your target market selection. Hot dogs make a great addition to store grand openings, school events, outdoor concerts, rodeos, craft shows, "Bike Night" at your local bars/restaurants, car shows / drive-ins, locally owned farm markets or grocery stores, music festivals, and auctions.

Competition

You must know who your competitors are and what they are charging for their products. The easiest way to identify competition is by using search engines on the internet as well as looking through the local yellow pages. Once you find out who your competitors are, you must perform market research. Market research is best conducted by calling your competitors and saying you would like to order a hot dog cart for a party you are hosting. You can also request a product list or check out the competition's website if there is one. Obtain several quotes so you get an idea of how much they are charging. Also inquire about their delivery and customer service process. Once you have a full list of competitors, describe their strengths and weaknesses and compare them to your company. This will be important when you are explaining to customers what sets your company apart from your competition. Remember, be close to your friends and be even closer to your enemies. We suggest you repeat this process every 6 months to identify new competition and to ensure your pricing strategy remains competitive.

Market Trends

You must identify industry trends (for the snack cart/food industry) and customer trends (see *"Target Market"* section earlier in this kit) every 6 months to ensure you are providing the right type of products and charging a fair price. Additionally, you need to take into account economic trends to determine if you can increase your price or if you need to decrease your price to become more competitive in the market.

Market Research

Market research can be completed through the following methods:
- Internet: use search engines to find the websites of your competitors. Identify how your competitors are advertising, what products they are selling, and how much they charge. Browse the websites of your competitors and identify what you like and what you dislike. When designing your website, make sure it looks professional because this will likely be the first way potential customers research your company and determine

if they want to rent a hot dog cart from your company. We suggest you hire a professional web designer to make sure your website looks as professional as possible. Make sure the web designer maximizes your website's exposure to internet search engines. You want to ensure your company is as visible as possible to potential customers who are conducting online research for hot dog cart companies in your geographic region. A professional website designer can be easily located by using an internet search engine.

- Yellow Pages: use the Yellow Pages to see which competitors are advertising in print. Based on the potential return on investment, you must determine if you want to advertise via the yellow pages or spend your advertising dollars elsewhere.
- Friends and Family: ask your friends and family members what they would want if they were looking for a hot dog cart company. Ask if they are more concerned with high quality hot dogs and a high level of service or if they would be more concerned with paying a low price. Ask at least 10 friends and family members to make sure you have a broad amount of market research to base your conclusions.
- Your Current Employer (Corporate): ask your current or previous employer who they use for hot dog cart services and how much they pay.

Marketing Strategy

General Description

Your marketing strategy should be tailored to your individual marketing strengths. Your marketing strategy should support your overall business strategy that was stated earlier under the "Summary Description of the Business" section.

Advertising Strategy

Your advertising strategy should consist of at least 4 of the below advertising media:
- Website: a website is mandatory for your business. A website provides the first impression that many potential customers will have about your company. If you have an unprofessional website, your chances of receiving a sales order will diminish. On the other hand, having a professional and informative website will add instant credibility to your company. Be sure to include pictures of your hot dog cart and a link to your e-mail address for questions like price and delivery inquiries. Discussing prices verbally will give you the opportunity to communicate your company strengths so you can persuade the customer to choose your company over the competition. Upstart Business Consulting Group has a team of website designers that are available to help build your website. Please click on the "*Services*" link on www.upstartbcg.com for more information.
- Search Engine Optimization: paying a company for search engine optimization will increase your website's exposure and can increase the number of hits to your website. Upstart Business Consulting Group has a team of SEO's that are available to help maximize your website's exposure. Please click on the "*Services*" link on www.upstartbcg.com for more information.
- Google AdWords: allows you to display your ads on Google and their advertising network. You can reach users searching

on Google or browsing websites in their content network, which can deliver your message to a targeted audience. You only pay if people click your ads. The Google content network comprises hundreds of thousands of high-quality websites, news pages, and blogs that partner with Google to display targeted AdWords ads. When you choose to advertise on the content network, you can expand your marketing reach to targeted audiences, and potential customers, visiting the content network sites every day.
- Yellow Pages (online or print): although the printed yellow pages are not as popular as they once were, they still provide a means for potential customers who lack internet savvy to find your company. However, if you would like to post an advertisement in the yellow pages, we suggest you post the advertisement online and forego the traditional yellow pages book that is printed and delivered to homes.
- Direct Mailers
    - Direct Mailers to Non-Profit Groups: create a list of non-profit groups in your target market by searching the internet, yellow pages, and community bulletin boards. Draft a letter to each group and introduce them to your products and services. Be sure to include a color brochure that has pictures of your hot dog cart. If they are interested in a fun fundraising opportunity, they will call you and request more information. You must convince them that your products can raise more money than their traditional fundraising techniques.
    - Direct Mailers to Party Planners: create a list of party planners in your target market by searching the internet and yellow pages. Draft a letter to each party planner and introduce them to your products. Be sure to include a color brochure that has pictures of your hot dog cart. One week after you mail your promotional material, call the party planner and ask if they have any questions. Explain your commission structure and give them an introduction to your company. Make a good first impression and do not be pushy. If you pressure the party planner, you will likely never hear back from them again.

- - Direct Mailers to Hotel Sales/Catering Manager: search the websites of all major hotel brands and create a list of hotels in your target market. Draft a letter to each sales/catering manager and introduce them to your products. Be sure to include a color brochure that has pictures of your hot dog cart. One week after you mail your promotional material, call the sales/catering department of each hotel and ask if they have any questions. Explain your commission structure and give them an introduction to your company. Make a good first impression and do not be pushy. If you pressure the sales/catering manager, you will likely never hear back from them again. If the hotel does not allow the sales/catering manager to receive a commission, then emphasize your high level of service and your quality products. If the sales/catering manager refers their customer to your company and you do a great job, the customer will be happy with the sales/catering manager and will continue to do business with that hotel. This is a win-win situation for both your company and the sales/catering manager.
  - Direct Mailers to Local Companies: create a list of local offices and businesses in your target market by searching the internet and yellow pages. Draft a letter to each company and introduce them to your products. Be sure to include a color brochure that has pictures of your hot dog cart. One week after you mail your promotional material, call the company and ask if they have any questions.
- Business Cards and other Promotional Materials at each event, make sure you have business cards readily available for customers to grab. All it takes is for the right person to take a $.05 business card and become a loyal customer a few months later. In addition to business cards, print brochures that provide a little more information about your company and your products and services. This small investment can pay off big with word of mouth marketing.
- Automobile Advertising: placing quality decals on your car's windows and sides can be an easy and low cost way of

advertising. Include your phone number, website, and e-mail address. This advertising is very direct as it will be viewed mainly by people living in your area. Be sure to check with your accountant for special tax rules regarding personal use of your vehicle for business advertising purposes.

Pricing

Pricing is a key component to the success of any business. If you price your products too high, you may lose a large segment of your market. If you price your products too low, you will attract customers who only care about price. You need to find a happy medium in your pricing strategy and build customer loyalty. Customer loyalty breeds word of mouth marketing. Word of mouth marketing is not only free, but it is also the most credible form of advertising. Once your company is established and word of mouth marketing spreads, you can spend less and less on traditional forms of advertising, thus increasing your profit margins.

In order to find out how much you should charge, you must find out how much your competition is charging. Refer to the "Market Analysis - Competition" section earlier for additional information.

If a customer asks you to reduce your price, always have a lowest acceptable price you are willing to accept. If this lowest acceptable price does not satisfy your customer, turn down the business. Explain to the customer that they will receive the type of service they pay for and you cannot reduce your price any further.

Brand

By definition, a brand is a name, term, sign, symbol, design, or a combination of these, intended to identify the goods or services of one seller or group of sellers and to differentiate them from those of competitors. Branding will add value to your company because your customers view a brand as an important part of the service. Your brand is perhaps the greatest intangible asset your company will possess. Your brand is going to determine the long term success of your business. If your brand is weak, you will likely see shrinking profit margins that will eventually crush your business. If your brand is built on value, great service, and high quality hot dogs, then you will see long term growth and business expansion.

Database Marketing

Customer satisfaction is great, but customer loyalty will make your business a long term success. With every new customer you receive, be sure to obtain specific information that you can use for database marketing. This information can include the customer's telephone number, e-mail address, home address, birth date, anniversary date, and other special occasion dates. You can then use this information to contact previous customers continually throughout the year. This will ensure your company stays fresh in their minds and will increase the likelihood that they will become loyal customers and spread the positive word of mouth. Always keep the database updated with current information.

Sales Strategy

You will have to learn how to sell your services to customers whether you like selling or not. Although you may be paralyzed by the thought that you will have to be a salesperson, the fact of the matter is that all entrepreneurs are salespeople. Selling is actually quite easy. All you really need to do is tell the customer what sets your company apart from your competition. Always be honest in your dealings and keep the sales message positive. Do not promise anything you cannot fulfill, as this is a sure way to create bad word of mouth.

Sales Incentives and Promotions

Sales promotions can be a great way to drum up business during slow times of the year. Sales promotions should be short-term incentives to encourage the purchase of your service. Whereas advertising and personal selling offer reasons to buy your service, sales promotions offer reasons to buy now. However, the ultimate goal is to have customers pay full price for your services. Relying on customers who always demand discounted prices will cheapen your brand and will ultimately ruin your business. We suggest you use the following types of sales promotions that will not cheapen your brand, but will increase customer loyalty:

- Cash Discount Based on Frequency: 10% discount on any 3 rentals in a single month (great for repeat corporate customers).
- Cash Donation: 10% donation (based on the total price of the sales) to non-profit groups who rent their hot dog cart through your company.

Public Relations

Public relations is the process of building good relations with the public (newspaper articles, TV news stories, etc.) by obtaining favorable publicity, building up a good image, and handling or heading off unfavorable rumors and stories.

A public relations campaign has its distinct advantages and disadvantages. The major advantage of public relations is that it provides free publicity for your company. However, since public relations exposure is free, you cannot control whether the exposure is favorable or unfavorable. Before any public relations campaign is implemented, you must first research how public relations will affect your company. Press releases should be made available to newspapers and television stations to promote your service. However, the more exposure you receive as a small company, the greater the threat of competition becomes as copy-cat entrepreneurs piggy back off your idea. It would be best to gain local exposure and brand recognition before you decide to pursue a public relations campaign. Since the barriers to entry are relatively low for this type of business, your strategy should be to artificially raise the barriers to entry by dominating market share and making it difficult for new competitors to capture market share from your company.

Networking

Networking is going to be vital to growing your business. Networking is inexpensive and credible. It gives you the opportunity to personally interact with potential customers and directly sell your service. Networking is an ongoing task because no matter where you are or who you are talking to, you can discuss your business. At minimum, use your closest network to start spreading positive word of mouth (i.e. family and friends). When your business is officially open, tell your family and friends about your business and what types of products and services you offer. Ask them to spread the word by telling their friends.

Another great networking tool is joining a referral association. There are plenty of referral associations to choose from. Use the internet to find local referral associations that you can join. A popular referral association is BNI (www.bni.com). Referral associations offer members the opportunity to share ideas, contacts, and business referrals. You are tasked with referring business to fellow members and they refer business to you. Since other members of your referral association are recommending your business, this type of indirect selling is highly credible. This is a proven strategy to growing your business.

Also, volunteering your services to fundraising events and participating in community activities will increase your networking opportunities.

Customer Service

Description of Customer Service Activities

Initially, you will be the only customer service specialist. All calls will be routed to your cell phone or a dedicated land line. Unless you are running this business full time, it is best to use a cell phone as your main business phone. Using a cell phone allows you to conduct business anytime, anywhere in the world.

As your business grows and you expand from a home-based business to a brick-and-mortar location, you may decide to hire an administrative assistant to perform the duties of the customer service specialist position. This will allow you focus your efforts on building your business instead of being bogged down with phone calls all day.

You must present a very professional appearance and provide the highest level of customer service possible whenever you are speaking to customers. If the customer calls with a question and receives your voicemail, be sure to call the customer back that day. If the customer e-mails you, reply to the e-mail within 4 hours. This commitment to customer service will breed long term customer loyalty and long term profits. Once revenues allow, you may decide to hire a part-time employee whose job responsibilities will include customer service.

Be sure your company is seen as being very professional. When meeting with potential customers, make sure you arrive on time, have a neat appearance, ask questions, and listen to your customer's needs. If you win the contract, make sure your hot dog cart arrives on time according to the contract schedule. Purchase uniforms and make sure workers adhere to your standard dress code to enhance your company's professional appearance.

Expected Outcomes of Achieving Excellence

The highest level of customer service is the only way to achieve long term growth and success. Your company cannot afford to have any unsatisfied customers, as bad word of mouth will eventually ruin your company. Also, if your customers remain happy, they will order from you in the future and provide positive word of mouth, thus lowering advertising expenditures in the future.

Implementation of Marketing Strategy

<u>In-house Responsibilities</u>

As with any startup, you will be responsible for implementing your marketing strategy. You will need to network heavily and use your network to spread positive word of mouth for your company. You will also need to create flyers or brochures that you can send out to non-profit organizations, hotels, party planners, local companies, and any other group you wish to market towards. Be sure to constantly update your marketing strategy based on what you find is working and what is not working.

<u>Outsourced Functions</u>

Outsourced marketing should only be considered if revenue and cash flow allow. Outsourced marketing functions include hiring an advertising agency, hiring graphic designers to create your marketing literature, and hiring a public relations firm to represent your company. These types of outsourced marketing and advertising functions are typically used by companies who have revenues in excess of $5,000,000 per year.

Assessment of Marketing Effectiveness

You need to make an assessment of how effective your marketing strategy is every 6 months. Calculate the return on investment (ROI) for each form of advertising media and redirect your marketing budget to the other forms of media which are generating the highest ROI. If an advertising media generates a negative ROI (meaning the cost of the media exceeds the profit the media generated), stop funding the media immediately.

Financial Documents

Financial Needs – Startup Expenses

You will need a budget of approximately $6,000 to start a hot dog cart company. The funds can be in the form of cash, credit cards, or loans. The following items represent the crucial equipment needed to start the company; a separate list is included for items necessary for future growth as your business matures.

Start up expenses:
- Equipment: 4,000: includes the following equipment:
    - Hot dog cart with the following specifications
        - Dimension - 40 in. wide x 48 in. long x 24 in. high
        - Dimensions on Trailer - 52 in. wide x 78 in. long x 56 in. high
        - Electrical - brake and signal lights plus trailer wiring harness installed
        - Cart Body - 18 Gauge Stainless Steel
        - Under Carriage - highway tires plus 1 caster wheel
        - Cart Weight - 350 lbs (160 Kg) approximately empty
        - Security - brass vibration proof cam locks
        - Sinks - 3 sinks standard, extra can be added
        - Fresh Water Tank - 5 gallons
        - Waste Water Tank - 7 gallons
        - Cooler Storage - insulated top entry ice box for up to 98 sodas plus meat
        - Dry Storage - top side display area plus additional under counter dry storage
        - Propane Tank - 2 x 20 lb tank baskets
        - Gas Regulator - two stage regulator
        - Burner - two 17,000 B.T.U burners with adjustable controls

- - Umbrella - 6-1/2 foot high wind umbrella
    - Steamers - 5 steamers pans 1/3 size x 6
    - Additional Standard Features - cart push handles, hot and cold running water
  - Bun warmer
  - Condiment dispensers
  - Foil bags
  - Napkin dispensers and napkins
  - Large tongs
- Insurance: $1,000 to $1,500: you will need both general liability insurance (for $1,000,000) and general property insurance. Refer to the "Insurance" section for additional information.
- Marketing: $500 to $1,000: refer to the "Marketing Strategy" section. Be sure to allocate your funds appropriately to maximize your return on investment.

Loan Dispersal Statement

Based on your cash on hand, you can disperse your loan or credit card funds as you see fit according to your startup budget. It is important not to grow too rapidly and outstrip your financing. Since the loan process can be tedious, you should really consider funding the business with credit cards if you do not have cash on hand. Once you start receiving positive cash flow, use 50% of the cash to fund growth and 50% of the cash to pay down your credit card debt. If you leverage your business too heavily with debt, you may never recover.

Credit Policy

You may decide to extend credit to frequent and trustworthy customers. However, you will want to collect most payments upon delivery to avoid the headache of tracking receivables that your customers owe you. If you do decide to extend credit to customers, send an invoice and allow your customers 30 days to pay the amount in full.

Business Bank Account

Some business owners open a separate business account with a bank to keep their personal and business expenses separate. This allows you to easily track income and expenses which enables you to evaluate your business' performance. If you would like to open up an account under the name of your business, you will need the following documents:

- Fictitious Business Name (DBA): if your business name is different from your personal name, you will be required to have a registered fictitious business name. You can file this at your county's Recorder Department for $20 to $80 per fictitious business name. To complete the registration process, you must announce your DBA to the public. This alerts the public that you are doing business under your DBA and not your personal name. Your county Recorder Department will have a list of local publications that will allow you to purchase an ad for several weeks so you can announce your DBA to the public. These ads typically cost less than $50.
- Employer Identification Number (EIN) (for partnerships and corporations only): you will need an EIN to provide to the bank. Obtaining an EIN is fast, easy, and free. Visit the IRS website at www.irs.gov and apply online. If you are not comfortable creating an EIN, Upstart Business Consulting Group has a team of consultants that are available to help setup your EIN. Please click on the "*Services*" link on www.upstartbcg.com for more information. If your business is a sole proprietorship, all you need is your Social Security number.
- Partnership Agreement (partnerships only): the bank will need a copy of your partnership agreement. Make sure the partnership agreement is signed by all partners. Refer to the sample partnership agreement on the template page of the UBCG website.
- LLC Operating Agreement (LLC only): the bank will need a copy of your LLC operating agreement. Refer to the sample LLC operating agreement on the template page of the UBCG website.
- Articles of Incorporation (S-Corporations and C-Corporations only): the bank will need a copy of your articles of

incorporation. Refer to the sample articles of incorporation on the template page of the UBCG website.

Break-even Analysis

The break-even point is the point at which a company's expenses exactly match the sales or service volume. It can be expressed in the following two ways:
- Total dollars or revenue exactly offset by total expenses, or
- Total units of production (cost of which exactly equals the income derived by their sales)

Since you are in the product industry, you will determine your breakeven point using the second calculation. This analysis can be done either mathematically or graphically. Revenue and expense figures are drawn from the income projections (refer to the "Three Year Income Statement Projection" section for income projections). See a detailed break-even formula in "Appendix A: Financial Ratios."

Tax Considerations

The type of business you operate determines the taxes you must pay and how you will pay them. There are four general kinds of business taxes.

Income Tax

Every business must file an annual income tax return. The form you use depends on the legal structure of your business. Income from your business is not subject to withholding. You typically pay the tax during the year as you earn your income. Sole proprietors, partners, or shareholders of an S-Corporation pay as they go by making regular tax payments based on the estimated annual tax for the year. If your independent contractors earn $600 or more in any given calendar year, you are also required to report their income to the IRS. It is the responsibility of the independent contractor to pay the required income taxes. Below is a breakdown detailing the various legal structures and what tax form you will need to file.

Legal Structure	IRS Form
Sole Proprietorship	Schedule C (Form 1040)
Partnership	Form 1065
Limited Liability Company	Schedule C (Form 1040)
S-Corporation	Form 1120S
C-Corporation	Form 1120 or 1120A

Forms and instructions for various types of business filings can be obtained for free at the Internal Revenue Service website (www.irs.gov).

Self-employment Tax

The self-employment tax is the Social Security tax for individuals who work for themselves, including sole proprietors and members of a partnership. The self-employment tax is figured and reported on Schedule SE, which is attached to and filed with Form 1040.

Employment Tax

If you have employees, you will probably be required to pay federal income tax withholding, Social Security and Medicare taxes, federal unemployment tax (Form 940 or Form 940EZ), and state income tax withholding.

Excise Tax

You may have to pay excise tax if you manufacture or sell certain products. Be sure to check with the federal, state, and local governments to identify excise taxes, permits, and licenses that may be required for your business.

Business License

A business license is a permit to sell a specific product or service in certain areas designated by state and local governments. Be sure to check with your city, county, and state governments regarding appropriate licensing requirements. Small business information can be obtained on most government websites or from the Small Business Administration website (www.sba.gov/hotlist/license.html).

Additionally, check with your local government agency to determine whether you need to purchase a vendor permit. The type of vendor permit may vary based on the type of event and location where you are selling your products. If you operate on private land, you may not need a vendor permit.

Outsourced Tax Functions

Outsourced tax functions can include taking your tax return to a professional Certified Public Accountant (CPA) to complete the filing. Unless you are a CPA, we suggest you take your annual income statement and a list of all valid business deductions to your CPA or tax preparer at the end of each year. This will ensure all income is appropriately reported.

Three Year Income Statement Projection

The income statement shows your business' financial activity (revenues and expenses) over a period of time, usually monthly and/or annually. It is a moving picture showing what has happened in your business and is an excellent tool for assessing your business' health. Once your ledger is closed, the net income or loss is transferred to the balance sheet in the owner's equity section. Note that most accounting software programs can calculate common financial statements for you after all the appropriate information is recorded. The following 3 pages provide sample income statement projections that will look similar to the income statement projections you will prepare when writing your business plan.

Upstart Business Consulting Group
www.upstartbcg.com
Income Statement - Year 1

	January Month 1	February Month 2	March Month 3	April Month 4	May Month 5	June Month 6	July Month 7	August Month 8	September Month 9	October Month 10	November Month 11	December Month 12	Year-to-date Total
Revenue													
Sales Revenue	$ 810	$ 2,955	$ 868	$ 1,960	$ 663	$ 875	$ 200	$ 4,200	$ 2,916	$ 1,140	$ 445	$ 3,887	$ 20,918
Other Sales (Advertising, etc.)	-	-	-	-	-	-	-	-	-	-	-	-	-
Total Revenue	810	2,955	868	1,960	663	875	200	4,200	2,916	1,140	445	3,887	20,918
Cost of Good Sold													
Direct Labor	243	887	260	588	199	263	60	1,260	875	342	134	1,166	6,276
Materials	20	20	20	20	20	20	20	20	20	20	20	20	240
Total Cost of Goods Sold	263	907	280	608	219	283	80	1,280	895	362	154	1,186	6,516
Gross Margin	547	2,049	588	1,352	444	593	120	2,920	2,021	778	292	2,701	14,403
Selling, General, Admin. Exp.													
Sales and Marketing	242	47	25	25	25	25	25	25	25	25	25	25	539
General & Administrative	128	95	95	95	95	95	95	95	95	95	95	95	1,175
Depreciation	122	122	122	122	122	122	122	122	122	122	122	122	1,467
Total SGA Expenses	491	264	242	242	242	242	242	242	242	242	242	242	3,180
Operating Income (Loss)	55	1,784	345	1,110	202	350	(122)	2,678	1,779	536	49	2,458	11,223
Interest Expense (Income)	-	-	-	-	-	-	-	-	-	-	-	-	-
Income (Loss) Before Taxes	55	1,784	345	1,110	202	350	(122)	2,678	1,779	536	49	2,458	11,223
Income Tax (Credit)	19	607	117	377	69	119	(42)	910	605	182	17	836	3,816
Income (Loss) After Taxes	$ 37	$ 1,177	$ 228	$ 732	$ 133	$ 231	$ (81)	$ 1,767	$ 1,174	$ 353	$ 32	$ 1,623	$ 7,407
Less: Distributions	-	-	-	-	-	-	-	-	-	-	-	-	-
Remaining Net Income	$ 37	$ 1,177	$ 228	$ 732	$ 133	$ 231	$ (81)	$ 1,767	$ 1,174	$ 353	$ 32	$ 1,623	$ 7,407

Upstart Business Consulting Group
www.upstartbcg.com
Income Statement - Year 2

	January Month 1	February Month 2	March Month 3	April Month 4	May Month 5	June Month 6	July Month 7	August Month 8	September Month 9	October Month 10	November Month 11	December Month 12	Year-to-date Total
Revenue													
Sales Revenue	$1,215	$4,433	$1,302	$2,940	$995	$1,313	$300	$6,300	$4,374	$1,710	$668	$5,831	$31,378
Other Sales (Advertising, etc.)	-	-	-	-	-	-	-	-	-	-	-	-	-
Total Revenue	1,215	4,433	1,302	2,940	995	1,313	300	6,300	4,374	1,710	668	5,831	31,378
Cost of Good Sold													
Direct Labor	364	1,330	391	882	298	394	90	1,890	1,312	513	200	1,749	9,413
Materials	30	75	75	75	75	75	-	75	75	75	75	75	780
Total Cost of Goods Sold	394	1,405	466	957	373	469	90	1,965	1,387	588	275	1,824	10,193
Gross Margin	820	3,028	836	1,983	621	844	210	4,335	2,987	1,122	392	4,006	21,184
Selling, General, Admin. Exp.													
Sales and Marketing	25	25	25	25	25	25	25	25	25	25	25	25	300
General & Administrative	95	95	95	95	95	95	95	95	95	95	95	95	1,143
Depreciation	122	122	122	122	122	122	122	122	122	122	122	122	1,467
Total SGA Expenses	242	242	242	242	242	242	242	242	242	242	242	242	2,909
Operating Income (Loss)	578	2,785	594	1,741	379	601	(32)	4,093	2,744	880	150	3,764	18,275
Interest Expense (Income)	-	-	-	-	-	-	-	-	-	-	-	-	-
Income (Loss) Before Taxes	578	2,785	594	1,741	379	601	(32)	4,093	2,744	880	150	3,764	18,275
Income Tax (Credit)	196	947	202	592	129	204	(11)	1,391	933	299	51	1,280	6,214
Income (Loss) After Taxes	$381	$1,838	$392	$1,149	$250	$397	$(21)	$2,701	$1,811	$581	$99	$2,484	$12,062
Less: Distributions	-	-	-	-	-	-	-	-	-	-	-	-	-
Remaining Net Income	$381	$1,838	$392	$1,149	$250	$397	$(21)	$2,701	$1,811	$581	$99	$2,484	$12,062

Upstart Business Consulting Group
www.upstartbcg.com

Income Statement - Year 3

	January Month 1	February Month 2	March Month 3	April Month 4	May Month 5	June Month 6	July Month 7	August Month 8	September Month 9	October Month 10	November Month 11	December Month 12	Year-to-date Total
Revenue													
Sales Revenue	$1,822	$6,649	$1,953	$4,410	$1,492	$1,969	$450	$9,450	$6,560	$2,565	$1,001	$8,746	$47,066
Other Sales (Advertising, etc.)	-	-	-	-	-	-	-	-	-	-	-	-	-
Total Revenue	1,822	6,649	1,953	4,410	1,492	1,969	450	9,450	6,560	2,565	1,001	8,746	47,066
Cost of Good Sold													
Direct Labor	547	1,995	586	1,323	448	591	135	2,835	1,968	770	300	2,624	14,120
Materials	30	75	75	75	75	75	-	75	75	75	75	75	780
Total Cost of Goods Sold	577	2,070	661	1,398	523	666	135	2,910	2,043	845	375	2,699	14,900
Gross Margin	1,245	4,579	1,292	3,012	969	1,303	315	6,540	4,517	1,721	626	6,047	32,166
Selling, General, Admin. Exp.													
Sales and Marketing	25	25	25	25	25	25	25	25	25	25	25	25	300
General & Administrative	95	95	95	95	95	95	95	95	95	95	95	95	1,143
Depreciation	122	122	122	122	122	122	122	122	122	122	122	122	1,467
Total SGA Expenses	242	242	242	242	242	242	242	242	242	242	242	242	2,909
Operating Income (Loss)	1,003	4,337	1,050	2,770	727	1,061	73	6,298	4,275	1,478	383	5,805	29,257
Interest Expense (Income)	-	-	-	-	-	-	-	-	-	-	-	-	-
Income (Loss) Before Taxes	1,003	4,337	1,050	2,770	727	1,061	73	6,298	4,275	1,478	383	5,805	29,257
Income Tax (Credit)	341	1,474	357	942	247	361	25	2,141	1,453	503	130	1,974	9,947
Income (Loss) After Taxes	$662	$2,862	$693	$1,828	$480	$700	$48	$4,156	$2,821	$976	$253	$3,831	$19,310
Less: Distributions	-	-	-	-	-	-	-	-	-	-	-	-	-
Remaining Net Income	$662	$2,862	$693	$1,828	$480	$700	$48	$4,156	$2,821	$976	$253	$3,831	$19,310

Three Year Balance Sheet Projection

The balance sheet shows your business' financial position (assets, liabilities, and owner's equity) over a period of time, usually monthly and/or annually. It is a moving picture showing what has happened in your business and is an excellent tool for assessing your business' health. Once your ledger is closed and balanced, the revenue and expense totals are transferred to this statement. The following 3 pages provide sample balance sheet statement projections that will look similar to the balance sheet statement projections you will prepare when writing your business plan.

Upstart Business Consulting Group
www.upstarfbcg.com
Balance Sheet - Year 1

	January Month 1	February Month 2	March Month 3	April Month 4	May Month 5	June Month 6	July Month 7	August Month 8	September Month 9	October Month 10	November Month 11	December Month 12
Assets												
Current Assets												
Cash & Cash Equivalents	$ 3,159	$ 4,458	$ 4,208	$ 5,063	$ 5,318	$ 5,707	$ 5,748	$ 7,637	$ 8,934	$ 9,409	$ 9,564	$ 11,309
Accounts Receivable	-	-	600	600	600	600	600	600	600	600	600	600
Inventory	-	-	-	-	-	-	-	-	-	-	-	-
Other Current Assets	-	-	-	-	-	-	-	-	-	-	-	-
Total Current Assets	3,159	4,458	4,808	5,663	5,918	6,307	6,348	8,237	9,534	10,009	10,164	11,909
Property & Equipment												
General Equipment	4,000	4,000	4,000	4,000	4,000	4,000	4,000	4,000	4,000	4,000	4,000	4,000
Automobile	4,000	4,000	4,000	4,000	4,000	4,000	4,000	4,000	4,000	4,000	4,000	4,000
Computer	800	800	800	800	800	800	800	800	800	800	800	800
Less: Accumulated Depreciation	(122)	(244)	(367)	(489)	(611)	(733)	(856)	(978)	(1,100)	(1,222)	(1,344)	(1,467)
Net Property & Equipment	8,678	8,556	8,433	8,311	8,189	8,067	7,944	7,822	7,700	7,578	7,456	7,333
Other Long-Term Assets	-	-	-	-	-	-	-	-	-	-	-	-
Total Long-Term Assets	8,678	8,556	8,433	8,311	8,189	8,067	7,944	7,822	7,700	7,578	7,456	7,333
Total Assets	$ 11,837	$ 13,014	$ 13,242	$ 13,974	$ 14,107	$ 14,373	$ 14,292	$ 16,060	$ 17,234	$ 17,587	$ 17,619	$ 19,242
Liabilities & Equity												
Current Liabilities												
Accounts Payable	$ 1,000	$ 1,000	$ 1,000	$ 1,000	$ 1,000	$ 1,000	$ 1,000	$ 1,000	$ 1,000	$ 1,000	$ 1,000	$ 1,000
Short-Term Borrowing	-	-	-	-	-	-	-	-	-	-	-	-
Other Current Liabilities	-	-	-	-	-	-	-	-	-	-	-	-
Total Current Liabilities	1,000	1,000	1,000	1,000	1,000	1,000	1,000	1,000	1,000	1,000	1,000	1,000
Long Term Debt	-	-	-	-	-	-	-	-	-	-	-	-
Other Long-Term Liabilities	-	-	-	-	-	-	-	-	-	-	-	-
Total Long-Term Liabilities	-	-	-	-	-	-	-	-	-	-	-	-
Total Liabilities	1,000	1,000	1,000	1,000	1,000	1,000	1,000	1,000	1,000	1,000	1,000	1,000
Owners Equity												
Owner's Investment (Contribution)	10,800	10,800	10,800	10,800	10,800	10,800	10,800	10,800	10,800	10,800	10,800	10,800
Retained Earnings - Prior Period	-	37	1,214	1,442	2,174	2,307	2,538	2,457	4,225	5,399	5,752	5,784
Retained Earnings - Current Period	37	1,177	228	732	133	231	(81)	1,767	1,174	353	32	1,623
Total Owners Equity	10,837	12,014	12,242	12,974	13,107	13,338	13,257	15,025	16,199	16,552	16,584	18,207
Total Liabilities & Equity	$ 11,837	$ 13,014	$ 13,242	$ 13,974	$ 14,107	$ 14,338	$ 14,257	$ 16,025	$ 17,199	$ 17,552	$ 17,584	$ 19,207

Upstart Business Consulting Group
www.upstartbcg.com
Balance Sheet - Year 2

	January Month 1	February Month 2	March Month 3	April Month 4	May Month 5	June Month 6	July Month 7	August Month 8	September Month 9	October Month 10	November Month 11	December Month 12
Assets												
Current Assets												
Cash & Cash Equivalents	$ 10,412	$ 10,914	$ 12,078	$ 12,595	$ 14,212	$ 15,403	$ 14,962	$ 16,396	$ 14,033	$ 15,260	$ 16,327	$ 15,327
Accounts Receivable	2,000	1,000	600	500	2,000	1,000	1,500	1,000	4,000	3,000	2,000	3,000
Inventory	-	-	-	-	-	-	-	-	-	-	-	-
Other Current Assets	-	-	-	-	-	-	-	-	-	-	-	-
Total Current Assets	12,412	11,914	12,678	13,095	16,212	16,403	16,462	17,396	18,033	18,260	18,327	18,327
Property & Equipment												
General Equipment	4,000	4,000	4,000	4,000	4,000	4,000	4,000	4,000	4,000	4,000	4,000	4,000
Automobile	4,000	4,000	4,000	4,000	4,000	4,000	4,000	4,000	4,000	4,000	4,000	4,000
Computer	800	800	800	800	800	800	800	800	800	800	800	800
Less: Accumulated Depreciation	(1,589)	(1,711)	(1,833)	(1,956)	(2,078)	(2,200)	(2,322)	(2,444)	(2,567)	(2,689)	(2,811)	(2,933)
Net Property & Equipment	7,211	7,089	6,967	6,844	6,722	6,600	6,478	6,356	6,233	6,111	5,989	5,867
Other Long-Term Assets	-	-	-	-	-	-	-	-	-	-	-	-
Total Long-Term Assets	7,211	7,089	6,967	6,844	6,722	6,600	6,478	6,356	6,233	6,111	5,989	5,867
Total Assets	$ 19,623	$ 19,003	$ 19,645	$ 19,939	$ 22,934	$ 23,003	$ 22,940	$ 23,752	$ 24,267	$ 24,371	$ 24,316	$ 24,193
Liabilities & Equity												
Current Liabilities												
Accounts Payable	$ 1,000	$ 1,000	$ 1,000	$ 1,000	$ 1,000	$ 1,000	$ 1,000	$ 1,000	$ 1,000	$ 1,000	$ 1,000	$ 1,000
Short-Term Borrowing	-	-	-	-	-	-	-	-	-	-	-	-
Other Current Liabilities	-	-	-	-	-	-	-	-	-	-	-	-
Total Current Liabilities	1,000	1,000	1,000	1,000	1,000	1,000	1,000	1,000	1,000	1,000	1,000	1,000
Long Term Debt	-	-	-	-	-	-	-	-	-	-	-	-
Other Long-Term Liabilities	-	-	-	-	-	-	-	-	-	-	-	-
Total Long-Term Liabilities	-	-	-	-	-	-	-	-	-	-	-	-
Total Liabilities	1,000	1,000	1,000	1,000	1,000	1,000	1,000	1,000	1,000	1,000	1,000	1,000
Owners Equity												
Owner's Investment (Contribution)	10,800	8,342	8,592	7,737	10,482	10,093	10,052	8,163	6,866	6,391	6,236	4,491
Retained Earnings - Prior Period	7,407	7,788	9,627	10,019	11,167	11,417	11,814	11,793	14,494	16,305	16,885	16,984
Retained Earnings - Current Period	381	1,838	392	1,149	250	397	(21)	2,701	1,811	581	99	1,623
Total Owners Equity	18,588	17,968	18,610	18,904	21,899	21,908	21,845	22,656	23,171	23,276	23,221	23,098
Total Liabilities & Equity	$ 19,588	$ 18,968	$ 19,610	$ 19,904	$ 22,899	$ 22,908	$ 22,845	$ 23,656	$ 24,171	$ 24,276	$ 24,221	$ 24,098

Upstart Business Consulting Group
www.upstarfbcg.com
Balance Sheet - Year 3

	January Month 1	February Month 2	March Month 3	April Month 4	May Month 5	June Month 6	July Month 7	August Month 8	September Month 9	October Month 10	November Month 11	December Month 12
Assets												
Current Assets												
Cash & Cash Equivalents	$ 18,702	$ 19,702	$ 20,702	$ 20,802	$ 22,302	$ 23,302	$ 22,802	$ 23,302	$ 20,302	$ 21,302	$ 22,302	$ 21,302
Accounts Receivable	2,000	1,000	600	500	2,000	1,000	1,500	1,000	4,000	3,000	2,000	3,000
Inventory	-	-	-	-	-	-	-	-	-	-	-	-
Other Current Assets	-	-	-	-	-	-	-	-	-	-	-	-
Total Current Assets	20,702	20,702	21,302	21,302	24,302	24,302	24,302	24,302	24,302	24,302	24,302	24,302
Property & Equipment												
General Equipment	4,000	4,000	4,000	4,000	4,000	4,000	4,000	4,000	4,000	4,000	4,000	4,000
Automobile	4,000	4,000	4,000	4,000	4,000	4,000	4,000	4,000	4,000	4,000	4,000	4,000
Computer	800	800	800	800	800	800	800	800	800	800	800	800
Less: Accumulated Depreciation	(122)	(244)	(367)	(489)	(611)	(733)	(856)	(978)	(1,100)	(1,222)	(1,344)	(1,467)
Net Property & Equipment	8,678	8,556	8,433	8,311	8,189	8,067	7,944	7,822	7,700	7,578	7,456	7,333
Other Long-Term Assets	-	-	-	-	-	-	-	-	-	-	-	-
Total Long-Term Assets	8,678	8,556	8,433	8,311	8,189	8,067	7,944	7,822	7,700	7,578	7,456	7,333
Total Assets	$ 29,380	$ 29,258	$ 29,735	$ 29,613	$ 32,491	$ 32,369	$ 32,247	$ 32,124	$ 32,002	$ 31,880	$ 31,758	$ 31,635
Liabilities & Equity												
Current Liabilities												
Accounts Payable	$ 1,000	$ 1,000	$ 1,000	$ 1,000	$ 1,000	$ 1,000	$ 1,000	$ 1,000	$ 1,000	$ 1,000	$ 1,000	$ 1,000
Short-Term Borrowing	-	-	-	-	-	-	-	-	-	-	-	-
Other Current Liabilities	-	-	-	-	-	-	-	-	-	-	-	-
Total Current Liabilities	1,000	1,000	1,000	1,000	1,000	1,000	1,000	1,000	1,000	1,000	1,000	1,000
Long Term Debt	-	-	-	-	-	-	-	-	-	-	-	-
Other Long-Term Liabilities	-	-	-	-	-	-	-	-	-	-	-	-
Total Long-Term Liabilities												
Total Liabilities	1,000	1,000	1,000	1,000	1,000	1,000	1,000	1,000	1,000	1,000	1,000	1,000
Owners Equity												
Owner's Investment (Contribution)	9,641	8,342	8,592	7,737	10,482	10,093	10,052	8,163	6,866	6,391	6,236	4,491
Retained Earnings - Prior Period	18,607	18,643	19,821	20,049	20,781	20,914	21,145	21,064	22,832	24,005	24,359	24,391
Retained Earnings - Current Period	37	1,177	228	732	133	231	(81)	1,767	1,174	353	32	1,623
Total Owners Equity	28,285	28,163	28,640	28,518	31,396	31,239	31,116	30,994	30,872	30,750	30,628	30,505
Total Liabilities & Equity	$ 29,285	$ 29,163	$ 29,640	$ 29,518	$ 32,396	$ 32,239	$ 32,116	$ 31,994	$ 31,872	$ 31,750	$ 31,628	$ 31,505

Three Year Cash Flow Projection

The cash flow statement projects what your business plan means in terms of dollars. It shows cash inflow and outflow over a period of time (usually monthly and/or annually) and is used for internal planning. If you are taking out a loan to fund your business, it is of prime interest to the lender and shows how you intend to repay your loan. Cash flow statements show both how much and when cash must flow in and out of your business. The following 3 pages provide sample cash flow statement projections that will look similar to the cash flow statement projections you will prepare when writing your business plan.

Upstart Business Consulting Group
www.upstartbcg.com

Cash Flow - Year 1

	January Month 1	February Month 2	March Month 3	April Month 4	May Month 5	June Month 6	July Month 7	August Month 8	September Month 9	October Month 10	November Month 11	December Month 12
Cash flows from operating activities:												
Net Income	$ 55	$ 1,784	$ 345	$ 1,110	$ 202	$ 350	$ (122)	$ 2,678	$ 1,779	$ 536	$ 49	$ 2,458
Adjustments to reconcile net income to net cash provided by operating activities (change in):												
Depreciation	122	122	122	122	122	122	122	122	122	122	122	122
Accounts Receivable	-	-	(600)	-	-	-	-	-	-	-	-	-
Other current assets	-	-	-	-	-	-	-	-	-	-	-	-
Accounts Payable	1,000	-	-	-	-	-	-	-	-	-	-	-
Other current liabilities	-	-	-	-	-	-	-	-	-	-	-	-
Other net cash inflows (outflows)	(19)	(607)	(118)	(377)	(68)	(84)	41	(910)	(604)	(183)	(16)	(836)
Net cash provided by (used in) operating activities	1,159	1,300	(251)	855	256	388	41	1,890	1,297	475	155	1,745
Cash flows from investing activities:												
Sale (Purchase) of Equipment	(8,800)	-	-	-	-	-	-	-	-	-	-	-
Net cash provided by (used in) investing activities	(8,800)	-	-	-	-	-	-	-	-	-	-	-
Cash flows from financing activities:												
Proceeds (payments) of short-term debt, net	-	-	-	-	-	-	-	-	-	-	-	-
Proceeds (payments) of long-term debt, net	-	-	-	-	-	-	-	-	-	-	-	-
Contributions (owner equity)	10,800	-	-	-	-	-	-	-	-	-	-	-
Distributions to owners & shareholders	-	-	-	-	-	-	-	-	-	-	-	-
Net cash provided by (used in) financing activities	10,800	-	-	-	-	-	-	-	-	-	-	-
Net increase (decrease) in cash and cash equivalents	3,159	1,300	(251)	855	256	388	41	1,890	1,297	475	155	1,745
Cash and cash equivalents at beginning of period	-	3,159	4,458	4,208	5,063	5,318	5,707	5,748	7,637	8,934	9,409	9,564
Cash and cash equivalents at end of period	$ 3,159	$ 4,458	$ 4,208	$ 5,063	$ 5,318	$ 5,707	$ 5,748	$ 7,637	$ 8,934	$ 9,409	$ 9,564	$ 11,309

Upstart Business Consulting Group
www.upstartbcg.com
Cash Flow - Year 2

	January Month 1	February Month 2	March Month 3	April Month 4	May Month 5	June Month 6	July Month 7	August Month 8	September Month 9	October Month 10	November Month 11	December Month 12
Cash flows from operating activities:												
Net Income	$ 1,215	$ 4,433	$ 1,302	$ 2,940	$ 995	$ 1,313	$ 300	$ 6,300	$ 4,374	$ 1,710	$ 668	$ 5,831
Adjustments to reconcile net income to net cash provided by operating activities (change in):												
Depreciation	122	122	122	122	122	122	122	122	122	122	122	122
Accounts Receivable	1,400	(1,000)	(400)	(100)	1,500	(1,000)	500	(500)	3,000	(1,000)	(1,000)	1,000
Other current assets	-	-	-	-	-	-	-	-	-	-	-	-
Accounts Payable	-	-	-	-	-	-	-	-	-	-	-	-
Other current liabilities	-	-	-	-	-	-	-	-	-	-	-	-
Other net cash inflows (outflows)	(3,633)	(595)	(110)	(1,591)	(3,744)	1,145	(1,322)	(2,599)	(8,563)	871	1,432	(6,208)
Net cash provided by (used in) operating activities	(896)	2,960	914	1,371	(1,127)	1,580	(399)	3,323	(1,067)	1,703	1,222	745
Cash flows from investing activities:												
Sale (Purchase) of Equipment	-	-	-	-	-	-	-	-	-	-	-	-
Net cash provided by (used in) investing activities	-	-	-	-	-	-	-	-	-	-	-	-
Cash flows from financing activities:												
Proceeds (payments) of short-term debt, net	-	-	-	-	-	-	-	-	-	-	-	-
Proceeds (payments) of long-term debt, net	-	-	-	-	-	-	-	-	-	-	-	-
Contributions (owner equity)	-	(2,458)	250	(855)	2,745	(388)	(41)	(1,889)	(1,296)	(476)	(155)	(1,745)
Distributions to owners & shareholders	-	-	-	-	-	-	-	-	-	-	-	-
Net cash provided by (used in) financing activities	-	(2,458)	250	(855)	2,745	(388)	(41)	(1,889)	(1,296)	(476)	(155)	(1,745)
Net increase (decrease) in cash and cash equivalents	(896)	501	1,164	517	1,617	1,191	(441)	1,434	(2,363)	1,228	1,067	(1,000)
Cash and cash equivalents at beginning of period	11,309	10,412	10,914	12,078	12,595	14,212	15,403	14,963	16,396	14,033	15,261	16,328
Cash and cash equivalents at end of period	$10,412	$10,914	$12,078	$12,595	$14,212	$15,403	$14,963	$16,396	$14,033	$15,261	$16,328	$15,328

Upstart Business Consulting Group
www.upstartbcg.com
Cash Flow - Year 3

	January Month 1	February Month 2	March Month 3	April Month 4	May Month 5	June Month 6	July Month 7	August Month 8	September Month 9	October Month 10	November Month 11	December Month 12
Cash flows from operating activities:												
Net Income	$ 1,822	$ 6,649	$ 1,953	$ 4,410	$ 1,492	$ 1,969	$ 450	$ 9,450	$ 6,560	$ 2,565	$ 1,001	$ 8,746
Adjustments to reconcile net income to net cash provided by operating activities (change in):												
Depreciation	122	122	122	122	122	122	122	122	122	122	122	122
Accounts Receivable	(1,000)	(1,000)	(400)	(100)	1,500	(1,000)	500	(500)	3,000	(1,000)	(1,000)	1,000
Other current assets	-	-	-	-	-	-	-	-	-	-	-	-
Accounts Payable	-	-	-	-	-	-	-	-	-	-	-	-
Other current liabilities	-	-	-	-	-	-	-	-	-	-	-	-
Other net cash inflows (outflows)	(2,719)	(3,471)	(925)	(3,478)	(4,358)	297	(1,531)	(6,683)	(11,386)	(212)	1,031	(9,123)
Net cash provided by (used in) operating activities	(1,775)	2,300	750	954	(1,244)	1,388	(459)	2,389	(1,703)	1,475	1,154	745
Cash flows from investing activities:												
Sale (Purchase) of Equipment	-	-	-	-	-	-	-	-	-	-	-	-
Net cash provided by (used in) investing activities	-	-	-	-	-	-	-	-	-	-	-	-
Cash flows from financing activities:												
Proceeds (payments) of short-term debt, net	-	-	-	-	-	-	-	-	-	-	-	-
Proceeds (payments) of long-term debt, net	-	-	-	-	-	-	-	-	-	-	-	-
Contributions (owner equity)	5,150	(1,300)	250	(855)	2,745	(388)	(41)	(1,889)	(1,296)	(476)	(155)	(1,745)
Distributions to owner's & shareholders	-	-	-	-	-	-	-	-	-	-	-	-
Net cash provided by (used in) financing activities	5,150	(1,300)	250	(855)	2,745	(388)	(41)	(1,889)	(1,296)	(476)	(155)	(1,745)
Net increase (decrease) in cash and cash equivalents	3,375	1,000	1,000	100	1,501	1,000	(500)	500	(2,999)	1,000	1,000	(1,000)
Cash and cash equivalents at beginning of period	15,327	18,702	19,702	20,702	20,802	22,302	23,302	22,802	23,302	20,302	21,302	22,302
Cash and cash equivalents at end of period	$18,702	$19,702	$20,702	$20,802	$22,302	$23,302	$22,802	$23,302	$ 20,302	$21,302	$ 22,302	$ 21,302

Additional Forecasting Charts

	January	February	March	April	May	June	July	August	September	October	November	December	Total
	Month 1	Month 2	Month 3	Month 4	Month 5	Month 6	Month 7	Month 8	Month 9	Month 10	Month 11	Month 12	
Year 1	810	2,955	868	1,960	663	875	200	4,200	2,916	1,140	445	3,887	20,918
Year 2	1,215	4,433	1,302	2,940	995	1,313	300	6,300	4,374	1,710	668	5,831	31,378
Year 3	1,822	6,649	1,953	4,410	1,492	1,969	450	9,450	6,560	2,565	1,001	8,746	47,066

Revenue Seasonality

Seasonality Trends

Depending on your type of business, you will encounter seasonal trends where sales will either increase or decrease. It is helpful to chart your sales so you can observe the seasonality trends of your specific business, which will help you make proper marketing decisions.

Revenue Growth by Year

Sales

Year	Sales
Year 1	~21,000
Year 2	~32,000
Year 3	~47,000

*Note that it is not unusual to experience 40% to 50% growth in your first few years of business when you are highly motivated, sufficiently market your products and/ or services, and continually build your customer base.

Supporting Documents

This section of your business plan will contain all of the records that back up the statements and decisions made in the main sections of your business plan. The most common supporting documents include:

Personal Resumes

Include resumes for owners and management. A resume should be a one-page document and include the following information:
- Work history
- Educational background
- Professional affiliations and honors
- Special skills relating to the company position

Refer to the sample personal resume on the template page of the UBCG website.

Owners Financial Statements

Include personal financial statements for each owner. The financial statement will show assets and liabilities held outside the business as well as personal net worth. Owners will often have to draw on personal assets to finance the business, and these statements will show what is available. Bankers and investors usually want this information as well. Refer to the sample personal financial statement on the template page of the UBCG website.

Credit Reports

You will need credit reports for each partner in the company. Credit reports can be received from any of the 3 major credit reporting agencies (Experian, Transunion, and Equifax). You can logon to www.annualcreditreport.com to access your credit reports from each of the 3 above credit reporting agencies once every 12 months. This service is free as required by federal law.

Copies of Leases, Mortgages, and other Agreements

All agreements currently in force between your company and a leasing agency, mortgage company, or other agency should be included here.

Letters of Reference

Letters recommending you as being a reputable and reliable business person worthy of being considered a good risk (both business and personal references). Letters of reference are particularly important when applying for a loan.

Contracts

Include all business contracts, both completed and currently in force.

Other Legal Documents

All legal papers pertaining to your legal structure, proprietary rights, insurance, shipping contracts, and all other legal documents.

Miscellaneous Documents

All other documents which have been referred to, but not included in the main body of the plan (e.g. location plans, demographics, competition analysis, advertising rate sheets, cost analysis, etc.).

Appendix A: Financial Ratios

Return on Investment (ROI)

$$\text{ROI} = \frac{(\text{Gain from Investment} - \text{Cost of Investment})}{\text{Cost of Investment}}$$

Return on Assets (ROA)

$$\text{ROA} = \frac{\text{Net Income}}{\text{Total Assets}}$$

Return on Equity (ROE)

$$\text{ROE} = \frac{\text{Net Income}}{\text{Average Shareholder Equity}}$$

Asset Turnover

$$\text{Asset Turnover} = \frac{\text{Sales}}{\text{Assets}}$$

Payback Period (in years)

$$\text{Payback Period} = \frac{\text{Initial Investment}}{\text{Annual Net Income}}$$

Appendix B: Helpful Websites

www.upstartbcg.com - Upstart Business Consulting Group home page, helpful templates for your business plan are available for free here. See login instructions at Appendix C.

www.annualcreditreport.com - Resource for obtaining credit reports for potential partners

www.bni.com - A popular referral association for generating customers

www.investopedia.com - Summary of financial ratios and information

www.irs.gov - Internal Revenue Service, useful for federal tax forms and rules

www.quickbooks.com - A website where you can purchase accounting software

www.sba.gov - United States Small Business Administration (SBA)

www.sba.gov/hotlist/license.html - State business license information

www.score.org - Service Corp of Retired Executives (SCORE)

www.taxcut.com - Software for preparing tax forms yourself

www.turbotax.com - Software for preparing tax forms yourself

www.usa.gov/Agencies/State_and_Territories.shtml - State government local websites and information

www.womma.org - Word of Mouth Marketing Association

Appendix C: Business Template Instructions

In order to access the free list of business templates, please log on to the Upstart Business Consulting Group website (www.upstartbcg.com) and browse to the secured "Templates" page. In order to gain access to the free business templates, you must input the following credentials:

User ID: UBCG
Password: Upstart1

Once you are granted access to the secured "Templates" page, click on the business template you want to download. A pop-up window will prompt you to save the file to your computer. Click the "save" button and select the location on your computer where you want to save the file. You can then reference the file on your own computer without logging in to the Upstart Business Consulting Group website.

Appendix D: Glossary

The glossary contains various terms that you may want to use when drafting your business plan.

Advertising - Any paid form of non-personal presentation and promotion of ideas, goods, or services by an identified sponsor

Advertising agency - A marketing services firm that assists companies in planning, preparing, implementing, and evaluating all or portions of their advertising programs

Advertising objective - A specific communication task to be accomplished with a specific target audience during a specific period of time

Asset turnover - Measures the efficiency of a company's use of its assets in generating sales revenue or sales income to the company

Baby boom - The significant increase in the annual birthrate following World War II and lasting until the early 1960s. The "baby boomers," now moving into middle age, are a prime target for marketers

Belief - A descriptive thought that a person holds about something

Benchmarking - The process of comparing the company's products and processes to those of competitors or leading firms in other industries to find ways to improve quality and performance

Bootstrap financing - Starting a business without the assistance of outside investors or additional debt. Examples include personal credit cards and savings

Brand - A name, term, sign, symbol, or design, or a combination of these intended to identify the goods or services of one seller or group of sellers and to differentiate them from those of competitors

Brand equity - The value of a brand, based on the extent to which it has high brand loyalty, name awareness, perceived quality, strong brand associations, and other assets such as patents, trademarks, and channel relationships

Brand extension - Using a successful brand name to launch a new or modified product in a new category

Break-even - The point at which total sales equals total costs. Net income equals zero

Business analysis - A review of the sales, costs, and profit projections for a new product to find out whether these factors satisfy the company's objectives

Buyer - The third party that exchanges consideration (money) for the products being sold

Buyer-readiness stages - The stages consumers normally pass through on their way to purchase, including awareness, knowledge, liking, preference, conviction, and purchase

By-product pricing - Setting a price for by-products in order to make the main product's price more competitive

Captive-product pricing - Setting a price for products that must be used along with an artificially low-priced main product, such as blades for a razor and film for a camera

Cash discount - A price reduction offered by companies to buyers who pay their bills promptly

Competition-based pricing - Setting prices based on the prices that competitors charge for similar products

Competitive advantage - An advantage over competitors gained by offering consumers greater value, either through lower prices or by providing more benefits that justify higher prices

Competitive marketing strategies - Strategies that strongly position the company against competitors and that give the company the strongest possible strategic advantage

Competitor analysis - The process of identifying key competitors; assessing their objectives, strategies, strengths and weaknesses, and reaction patterns; and selecting which competitors to attack or avoid

Consumer buying behavior - The buying behavior of final consumers- individuals and households who buy goods and services for personal consumption

Contests, sweepstakes, games - Promotional events that give consumers the chance to win something by luck or through extra effort (e.g. cash, trips, or something else a consumer may value)

Core competency - An organization's major value creating skills, capabilities, and resources that determine its competitive weapons

Cost of goods sold - The net cost to the company of goods sold

Cost-plus pricing - Adding a standard markup to the cost of the product

Coupon - Certificate that gives buyers a saving when they purchase a specified product

Credibility - When customers perceive you as being honest and competent

Current ratio - Measure of the business' liquidity and how easily the company can pay current term debts

Customer lifetime value - The amount by which revenues from a given customer over time will exceed the company's costs of attracting, selling, and servicing that customer

Customer sales force structure - A sales force organization under which salespeople specialize in selling only to certain customers or industries

Customer satisfaction - The extent to which a product's perceived performance matches a buyer's expectations. If the product's performance falls short of expectations, the buyer is dissatisfied. If performance matches or exceeds expectations, the buyer is satisfied or delighted

Deciders - People in the organization's buying center who have formal or informal power to select or approve the final suppliers

Demand curve - A curve that shows the number of units the market will buy in a given time period at different prices that might be charged

Demands - Human wants that are backed by buying power

Demographic segmentation – Dividing the market into groups based on demographic variables such as age, gender, family size, family life cycle, income, occupation, education, religion, race, and nationality

Differentiated marketing - A market-coverage strategy in which a firm decides to target several market segments and designs separate offers for each

Direct marketing - Direct communications with carefully targeted individual consumers to obtain an immediate response, and cultivate lasting customer relationships

Direct marketing channel - A marketing channel that has no intermediary levels

Direct-mail marketing - Direct marketing through single mailings that include letters, ads, samples, foldouts, and other "salespeople with wings" sent to prospects on mailing lists

Discount - A straight reduction in price on purchases during a stated period of time

Electronic commerce (e-commerce) - The general term for a buying and selling process that is supported by electronic means

Employer Identification Number (EIN) - A unique nine-digit number assigned by the Internal Revenue Service (IRS) to businesses operating in the United States for the purposes of identification. Such number is required to open a bank account at a financial institution in the name of the business. This number can be obtained for free by visiting www.irs.gov

Entrepreneurship - A process by which people pursue opportunities, fulfilling needs and wants through innovation, without regard to the resources they currently control

Federal Insurance Contributions Act (FICA) - A United States payroll (or employment) tax imposed by the federal government on both employees and employers to fund Social Security and Medicare (federal programs that provide benefits for retirees, the disabled, and children of deceased workers). Social Security benefits include old-age, survivors, and disability insurance (OASDI). Medicare provides hospital insurance benefits

Fictitious Business Name (Doing Business As or "DBA") - This is a legal phrase in which the name of the business or operation does not include the owner's name, partners' names, or other identifying names. A DBA is required to open a bank account at a financial institution in the name of the business

Fixed costs - Costs that do not vary with production or sales level

Forecasting - The art of estimating future demand by anticipating what buyers are likely to do under a given set of conditions

Franchise - A contractual association between a manufacturer, wholesaler, or service organization (a franchiser) and independent businesspeople (franchisees) who buy the right to own and operate one or more units in the franchise system

Franchise organization - A contractual vertical marketing system in which a channel member, called a franchiser, links several stages in the production-distribution process

Functional discount - A price reduction offered by the seller to trade channel members who perform certain functions such as selling, storing, and recordkeeping

General need description - The stage in the business buying process in which the company describes the general characteristics and quantity of a needed item

Geographic segmentation - Dividing a market into different geographical units such as nations, states, regions, counties, cities, or neighborhoods

Gross margin - The amount of contribution to the business enterprise, after paying for direct fixed and variable unit costs (Gross Profit = Revenue − Cost of Goods Sold

Gross sales - The total amount that a company charges during a given period of time for merchandise

Group - Two or more people who interact to accomplish individual or mutual goals

Growth stage - The product life-cycle stage in which a product's sales start climbing quickly

Income segmentation - Dividing a market into different income groups

Indirect marketing channel - Channel containing one or more intermediary levels

Individual marketing - Tailoring products and marketing programs to the needs and preferences of individual customers. Individual marketing is also know as customized marketing, one-to-one marketing, and markets-of-one-marketing

Influencers - People in an organization's buying center who affect the buying decision. Influencers often help define specifications and also provide information for evaluating alternatives

Information search - The stage of the buyer decision process in which the consumer is aroused to search for more information. The consumer may simply have heightened attention or may go into active information search

Integrated direct marketing - Direct-marketing campaigns that use multiple vehicles and multiple stages to improve response rates and profits

Integrated marketing communications (IMC) - The concept under which a company carefully integrates and coordinates its many communications channels to deliver a clear, consistent, and compelling message about the organization and its products

Internal databases - Computerized collections of information obtained from data sources within the company

Internal marketing - Marketing by a service firm to train and effectively motivate its customer-contact employees and all the supporting service people to work as a team to provide customer satisfaction

Job description - A written statement of what a jobholder does, how it is done, and why it is done

Leading indicators - Time series that change in the same direction but in advance of company sales

Licensing - A method of entering a foreign market in which the company enters into an agreement with a licensee in the foreign market, offering the right to use a manufacturing process, trademark, patent, trade secret, or other item of value for a fee or royalty

Local marketing - Tailoring brands and promotions to the needs and wants of local customer groups (e.g. cities, neighborhoods, and even specific stores)

Macroenvironment - The larger societal forces that affect the microenvironment (i.e. demographic, economic, natural, technological, political, and cultural forces)

Markdown - A percentage reduction from the original selling price

Market - The set of all actual and potential buyers of a product or service

Market-centered company - A company that pays balanced attention to both customers and competitors in designing its marketing strategies

Market development - A strategy for company growth by identifying and developing new market segments for current company products

Market follower - A runner-up firm in an industry that wants to hold its share without rocking the boat

Market leader - The firm in an industry with the largest market share. The market leader usually leads other firms in price changes, new product introductions, distribution coverage, and promotion spending

Market penetration - A strategy for company growth by increasing sales of current products to current market segments without changing the product

Market-penetration pricing - Setting a low price for a new product in order to attract a large number of buyers and a large market share

Market positioning - Arranging for a product to occupy a clear, distinctive, and desirable place relative to competing products in the minds of target consumers. Formulating competitive positioning for a product and a detailed marketing mix

Market potential - The upper limit of market demand

Market segment - A group of consumers who respond in a similar way to a given set of marketing efforts

Market segmentation - Dividing a market into distinct groups of buyers on the basis of needs, characteristics, or behaviors who might require separate products or marketing mixes

Market-skimming pricing - Setting a high price for a new product to skim maximum revenues layer by layer from the segments willing to pay the high price. The company makes fewer but more profitable sales

Market targeting - The process of evaluating each market segment's attractiveness and selecting one or more segments to enter

Marketing - A social and managerial process whereby individuals and groups obtain what they need and want through creating and exchanging products and value with others

Marketing communications mix (promotion mix) - The specific mix of advertising, personal selling, sales promotion, public relations, and direct marketing a company uses to pursue its advertising and marketing objectives

Marketing control - The process of measuring and evaluating the results of marketing strategies and plans, and taking corrective action to ensure that marketing objectives are achieved

Marketing implementation - The process that turns marketing strategies and plans into marketing actions in order to accomplish strategic marketing objectives

Marketing intermediaries - Firms that help the company to promote, sell, and distribute its goods to final buyers. Marketing intermediaries include resellers, physical distribution firms, marketing service agencies, and financial intermediaries

Marketing management - The analysis, planning, implementation, and control of programs designed to create, build, and maintain beneficial exchanges with target buyers for the purpose of achieving organizational objectives

Marketing mix - The set of controllable tactical marketing tools (i.e. product, price, place, and promotion) that the firm blends to produce the response it wants in the target market

Marketing process - The process of (1)analyzing marketing opportunities, (2)selecting target markets, (3)developing the marketing mix, and (4)managing the marketing effort

Marketing research - The systematic design, collection, analysis, and reporting of data relevant to a specific marketing situation facing an organization

Markup - The percentage of the cost or price of a product added to the cost in order to arrive at a selling price

Microenvironment - The forces close to the company that affect its ability to serve its customers (e.g. the company, suppliers, marketing channel firms, customer markets, competitors, and publics)

Mission statement - A statement of the organization's purpose and what it wants to accomplish in the larger environment

Need - A state of felt deprivation

Need recognition - The first stage of the buyer decision process in which the consumer recognizes a problem or need

Niche marketing - Focusing on sub segments or niches with distinctive traits that may seek a special combination of benefits

Online ads - Ads that appear while subscribers are surfing online services or Web sites, including banners and pop-up windows

Online databases - Computerized collections of information available from online commercial sources or via the internet

Online marketing - Marketing conducted through interactive online computer systems, which link consumers with sellers electronically

Operating income - The amount of income left after reducing gross margin (sales minus cost of goods sold) by general operating expenses such as depreciation, selling, and administrative expenses

Opportunity - Positive external factors that a company can exploit

Packaging - The activities of designing and producing the container or wrapper for a product

Patronage reward - Cash or other award for the regular use of a certain company's products or services

Pay-back period - The time period at which the initial investment is fully recovered. This can be measured in days, months, or years

Perception - The process by which people select, organize, and interpret information to form a meaningful picture of the world

Personal selling - Personal presentation by the firm's sales force for the purpose of making sales and building customer relationships

Physical distribution (marketing logistics) - The tasks involved in planning, implementing, and controlling the physical flow of materials, final goods, and related information from points of origin to points of consumption to meet customer requirements at a profit

Point-of-purchase (POP) promotion - Display and demonstration that takes place at the point of purchase or sale

Premium - Good offered either free or at low cost as an incentive to buy a product

Presentation - The step in the selling process in which the salesperson tells the product "story" to the buyer, showing how the product will make or save money for the buyer

Price - The amount of money charged for a product or service, or the sum of the values that consumers exchange for the benefits of having or using the product or service

Price elasticity - A measure of the sensitivity of demand to changes in price

Price pack (cents-off deal) - Reduced price that is marked by the producer directly on the label or package

Primary demand - The level of total demand for all brands of a given product or service (e.g. the total demand for toothbrushes)

Product - Anything that can be offered to a market for attention, acquisition, use, or consumption that might satisfy a want or need. It includes physical objects, services, events, persons, places, organizations, and ideas

Product bundle pricing - Combining several products and offering the bundle at a reduced price

Product concept - The idea that consumers will favor products that offer the most quality, performance, and features and that the organization should therefore devote its energy to making continuous product improvements. A detailed version of the new product idea stated in meaningful consumer terms

Product development - A strategy for company growth by offering modified or new products to current market segments. Developing the product concept into a physical product in order to ensure that the product idea can be turned into a workable product

Product life cycle (PLC) - The course of a product's sales and profits over its lifetime. It involves five distinct stages: product development, introduction, growth, maturity, and decline

Product mix (or product assortment) - The set of all product lines and items that a particular seller offers for sale

Product position - The way the product is defined by consumers on important attributes (i.e. the place the product occupies in consumers' minds relative to competing products)

Product quality - The ability of a product to perform its functions, including the product's overall durability, reliability, precision, ease of operation and repair, and other valued attributes

Profit margin - The measure of profitability (Revenue / Net Income)

Promotional pricing - Temporarily pricing products below the list price, and sometimes even below cost, to increase short-run sales

Prospecting - The step in the selling process in which the salesperson identifies qualified potential customers

Psychographic segmentation - Dividing a market into different groups based on social class, lifestyle, or personality characteristics

Psychological pricing - A pricing approach that considers the psychology of prices and not simply the economics. The price is used to say something about the product

Public relations - Building good relations with the company's various publics by obtaining favorable publicity, building up a good image, and handling or heading off unfavorable rumors, stories, and events. Major PR tools include press relations, product publicity, corporate communications, lobbying, and public service

Push strategy - A promotion strategy that calls for using the sales force and trade promotion to push the product through channels. The producer promotes the product to wholesalers, the wholesalers promote to retailers, and the retailers promote to consumers

Quality - The totality of features and characteristics of a product or service that bear on its ability to satisfy stated or implied needs

Quantity discount - A price reduction to buyers who buy large volumes

Quick ratio (acid test ratio) - Measure of the business' liquidity, excluding inventory

Reference prices - Prices that buyers carry in their minds and refer to when they look at a given product

Relationship marketing - The process of creating, maintaining, and enhancing strong, value-laden relationships with customers and other stakeholders

Return on assets (ROA) - The Return on Assets (ROA) percentage shows how profitable a company's assets are in generating revenue

Return on equity (ROE) - Measures the rate of return on the ownership interest (shareholders' equity) of the common stock owners

Return on investment (ROI) - A common measure of managerial effectiveness (i.e. the ratio of net profit to investment)

Risk - Those conditions in which the decision maker is able t o estimate the likelihood of certain outcomes

Sales promotion - Short-term incentives to encourage the purchase or sale of a product or service

Sample - A segment of the population selected for marketing research to represent the population as a whole. A sample is typically a trial amount of the product

Seasonal discount - A price reduction to buyers who purchase merchandise or services out of season

Selling process - The steps that the salesperson follows when selling, which include prospecting and qualifying, pre-approach, approach, presentation and demonstration, handling objections, closing, and follow-up

Service - Any activity or benefit that one party can offer to another that is essentially intangible and does not result in the ownership of anything

Slotting fees - Payments demanded by retailers before they will accept new products and find available space (i.e. slots) for the products on the shelves

Social marketing - The design, implementation, and control of programs seeking to increase the acceptability of a social idea, cause, or practice among a target group

Societal marketing concept - The idea that the organization should determine the needs, wants, and interests of target markets and deliver the desired satisfactions more effectively and efficiently than do competitors in a way that maintains or improves the consumer's and society's well-being

Specialty product - Consumer product with unique characteristics or brand identification for which a significant group of buyers is willing to make a special purchase effort

Strategic planning - The process of developing and maintaining a strategic fit between the organization's goals and capabilities and its changing marketing opportunities. It involves defining a clear company mission, setting supporting objectives, designing a sound business portfolio, and coordinating functional strategies

Strengths - Activities the firm does well or resources it controls

Supplier search - The stage of the business buying process in which the buyer tries to find the best vendors

Supplier selection - The stage of the business buying process in which the buyer reviews proposals and selects a supplier

Target market - A set of buyers sharing common needs or characteristics that the company decides to serve

Team selling - Using teams of people from sales, marketing, engineering, finance, technical support, and even upper management to service large, complex accounts

Test marketing - The stage of new product development in which the product and marketing program are tested in more realistic market settings

Third-party logistics provider - An independent logistics provider that performs any or all of the functions required to get its customers' product to market

Threat - Negative external environmental factors that a company cannot exploit

Total costs - The sum of the fixed and variable costs for any given level of production

Total customer cost - The total of all the monetary, time, energy, and psychic costs associated with a marketing offer

Total market demand - The total volume of a product or service that would be bought by a defined consumer group in a defined geographic area in a defined time period in a defined marketing environment under a defined level and mix of industry marketing effort

Uniform-delivered pricing - A geographical pricing strategy in which the company charges the same price plus freight to all customers, regardless of their location

Users - Members of the organization who will use the product or service. Users often initiate the buying proposal and help define product specifications

Value analysis - An approach to cost reduction in which components are studied carefully to determine if they can be redesigned, standardized, or made by less costly methods of production

Value-based pricing - Setting price based on buyers' perceptions of value rather than on the seller's cost

Value pricing - Offering just the right combination of quality and good service at a fair price

Variable costs - Costs that vary directly with the level of production

Want - The form taken by a human need as shaped by culture and individual personality

Weaknesses - Activities the firm does not do well or resources it needs but does not possess

<u>Wholesaling</u> - All activities involved in selling goods and services to those buying for resale or business use

<u>Word-of-mouth influence</u> - Personal communication about a product between target buyers and neighbors, friends, family members, and associates

Made in the USA
Columbia, SC
10 August 2023